W9-DBE-851

John
Muir

PIONEERS in CHANGE

W h 3

12/91

DISCARD

JB
MUIR

John Muir

EDEN FORCE

Silver Burdett Press
Englewood Cliffs, New Jersey

The author dedicates this book to Robert, Blake, and Devra.

CONSULTANTS:

Robert Fry
Yosemite National Park
Division of Interpretation

Richard M. Haynes
Assistant Professor
Division of Administration, Curriculum,
and Instruction
Western Carolina University

PHOTOGRAPH ACKNOWLEDGMENTS:
Courtesy: The Bancroft Library: pp. ii, 115, 121, 131, 134; John Muir Papers, Holt-Atherton Center for Western Studies, University of the Pacific. Copyright 1984 Muir-Hanna Trust: pp. 3, 24, 32, 41, 57, 66, 70, 81, 103, 112, 119, 127; State Historical Society of Wisconsin: 37.

SERIES AND COVER DESIGN:
R STUDIO T Raúl Rodríguez and Rebecca Tachna

ART DIRECTOR:
Linda Huber

MANAGING EDITOR
Nancy Furstinger

PROJECT EDITOR:
Richard G. Gallin

PHOTO RESEARCH:
Omni-Photo Communications, Inc.

Copyright © 1990 by Gallin House Press, Inc.
All rights reserved including the right of reproduction
in whole or in part in any form.

Published by Silver Burdett Press, Inc., a division of
Simon & Schuster, Inc., Englewood Cliffs, NJ 07632

Library of Congress Cataloging-in-Publication Data

Eskin, Eden Force.
John Muir / Eden Force.
p.   cm.—(Pioneers in change)
Includes bibliographical references.
Summary: A biography of the naturalist who, among other activities, founded the
Sierra Club and, as an early proponent of wilderness preservation, was influential in
establishing the national park service.
1. Muir, John, 1838-1914—Juvenile literature.   2. Naturalists—United States—
Biography—Juvenile literature.
3. Conservationists—United States—Biography—Juvenile literature.
[1. Muir, John, 1838-1914.   2. Naturalists.   3. Conservationists.]
I. Title.   II. Series.
QH31.M9E84   1990
333.7′2′092—dc20
[B]   90-34464
[92]   CIP
                                       AC

Manufactured in the United States of America.
ISBN 0-382-09965-6 [lib. bdg.]
10 9 8 7 6 5 4 3 2 1
ISBN 0-382-09970-2 [pbk.]
10 9 8 7 6 5 4 3 2 1

CONTENTS

1

Scotland, School, and Scootchers

The haunted ruins of Dunbar Castle overlook the fishing town of Dunbar, Scotland. The castle was built more than a thousand years ago to protect the people from waves of invaders who wanted to sail up the Firth of Forth, an inlet of the sea, and raid Scotland. Now the castle at the southern shore of the Firth was in ruins. That made it a favorite playground for adventurous local boys. Other customary play areas were the harbor and the open fields around the city.

One of the boys who made the castle, harbor, and fields a playground was John Muir, the son of Daniel Muir, a fairly prosperous food and grain dealer, and his wife, Anne.

Daniel Muir had not always been well-to-do. He was orphaned when he was only six years old and had to live with relatives. Many years later, John described his father's early years as that of a "farm servant" who worked for his sister and brother-in-law until he ran away hoping to go to

America. Young Daniel fled to Glasgow and tried to find work that would allow him to earn the money he needed for a ship ticket to America. But the only work he could find was in the army. He became a soldier, and eventually the army sent Daniel to Dunbar as a recruiting sergeant.

Daniel Muir was tall and handsome. Soon after he arrived in Dunbar, he went to the kirk, or church. There he joined in the worship and enjoyed singing hymns in his beautiful voice. It wasn't long before several women in the kirk began to notice him. One of them had inherited a food and grain enterprise, but she hadn't been trained to operate it and had trouble keeping the business prosperous. Daniel married her. Soon afterward she paid for her husband's release from the army so that he could take over the enterprise. His good business sense as well as his reputation for honesty made it thrive. Unfortunately, Daniel's wife died about a year after their marriage.

The Gilrye (pronounced gill RIE) family lived diagonally across the street from the house in which Daniel Muir had his home and business. Of the ten Gilrye children, only two daughters—Margaret and Anne—had survived past childhood. Margaret was married. Anne spent some of her time painting and doing embroidery and needlework.

Shortly after his wife's death, Daniel Muir began courting Anne Gilrye. Mr. Gilrye was concerned about what he considered to be Daniel's religious fanaticism. Nevertheless, Daniel and Anne were married in 1833.

The couple lived in a house that was bought from a Dr. Wrightman. Daniel's business was on the street floor, and his family lived on the floors above. The new Mrs. Muir quickly learned that her husband's religious beliefs affected the household. He belonged to a newly formed religious group called Campbellites, rather than to the Scottish Presbyterian

John Muir's birthplace, Dunbar, Scotland.

state church. Anne Muir wasn't allowed to hang pictures on the walls or to display embroidery. Daniel believed these things were evil because the Bible said "Thou shalt not make unto thee any graven images." However, Anne didn't protest. Scottish wives were expected to obey their husbands.

In place of the works of art she wasn't permitted to display, Anne Muir decorated her home with an abundance of flowers. The Muirs had a beautiful garden behind the house. It was surrounded by a high wall that kept intruders out. Anne's sister, Margaret, had a special corner of the garden in which she grew lilies.

The Muirs' first two children were daughters, Margaret and Sarah. Then, on April 21, 1838, John, their first son, was born. About two years later, David was born. He would

3

become John's closest friend and playmate for many years.

John grew very protective of his younger brother and remained so for many years. When a doctor gave David a vaccination shot, John bit the doctor's arm. "I wanna gan to let him hurt my bonnie brither," John declared, meaning, "I wasn't going to let him hurt my fine brother."

Among John's earliest memories were the sounds of his father playing the fiddle and singing. Daniel Muir made his own fiddle when he was a boy and taught himself to play it. He loved to sing Scottish ballads—songs that told stories of Scottish heroes. Many had fought and died for Scotland, some near the town of Dunbar. After a while, however, Daniel stopped singing ballads because he thought they weren't sufficiently religious. Instead, he sang hymns.

Grandfather Gilrye spent a lot of time with little John. Together they walked through the town as Grandfather taught John to recognize first the letters they saw printed on the shop signs and then the words. Using the big town clocks that fascinated John, Grandfather also taught him numbers.

As John's legs grew stronger, he and Grandfather Gilrye ventured out into the countryside. On one of these walks they had stopped to sit in a hayfield when John heard a "prickly, stinging cry." His grandfather had heard nothing, but when John looked through the hay he found a mother mouse with a half-dozen babies. He later recalled this as "a wonderful discovery." Although he was only about three at the time, John still remembered this incident when he grew old. Perhaps it was here that he first became aware of a love of animals that would stay with him all his life.

One morning when John was barely three, his father announced that he would begin school that day. His mother dressed him in a plaid kilt with a red petticoat underneath and placed a green book bag with a primer over his shoulder.

Then his sisters took him to the primary school at the foot of a hill called Davel Brae.

Much to John's embarrassment, he lost his red petticoat just before recess on that first day. Mungo Siddons, the *dominie*, or teacher, held it up and asked who had lost it. John, who was too embarrassed to claim it, said nothing. Then an older boy called out, "It's Johnny Moor's. I saw him drap it." John was mortified, but he had to go up in front of the class and claim his petticoat.

School was very strict, as the parents expected it to be. Although the boys spoke Scottish at home and in the streets, their lessons were taught in English. Before long, the boys were able to switch back and forth between Scottish and English. Mungo Siddons used threats and whippings to get his students to learn their lessons. At that time, many people believed that children would learn nothing unless it was beaten into them.

The schoolboys fought in the school yard whenever they could. They looked forward to these fights. Each boy wanted to gain a reputation as a "gude fechter," or good fighter. They wanted to be like the heroes of the Scottish ballads.

John's school days began to fall into a pattern. He got up and ate his breakfast of oatmeal with milk or treacle (molasses). After breakfast it was off to school. By noon, when he came home, he was very hungry. Like all the family's meals, midday dinner, the big meal of the day, was cooked in the fireplace. Dinner usually consisted of broth, a small piece of boiled mutton, and a barley scone—a kind of biscuit. Often the meal was barely enough to satisfy the children's hunger, but the only seconds they were permitted was the barley scone—the food they liked the least. Although the family had enough money for food, Daniel Muir didn't believe in "spoiling" his children with too much food or with food that was costly. The family always said grace before a meal and ate in silence. Because Daniel considered all meals to be a sacrament, no one was allowed to talk at the table.

After the midday dinner it was back to school. Tea was served to the children when they came home at the end of the school day. This was a kind of snack made up of a half slice of unbuttered bread, another barley scone, and "content"—a drink of warm water with a small amount of milk and sugar. John described content as being warming but not cheering.

For John (and David, too, when he joined John at school) the best part of the day came after school was over. Then the brothers would go across the street to visit their grandparents. Grandfather Gilrye enjoyed hearing the boys recite their lessons, and he helped them memorize what they needed to learn. Grandmother Gilrye pampered them with special cookies and cakes. Afterward they returned home to a boiled potato and another scone. Daniel Muir then held a family worship, and the children were sent to bed.

If the children's dominie was strict, their father was even stricter. In addition to school lessons, the boys had to learn Bible lessons at home. Daniel Muir made his sons learn hymns and a few verses of the Bible each day. He whipped them whenever they failed to memorize their Bible verses. Whenever she could, Anne Muir reminded her sons in time to help them avoid a whipping. John was lucky. He had an excellent memory and learned his verses fairly easily. By the time he was eleven, John could recite all of the New Testament and about three-quarters of the Old Testament "by heart and by sore flesh." Later in life, he would find his knowledge of the Bible very helpful.

When John was about seven or eight, he was sent to the local grammar school. The Dunbar Grammar School was in a building that looked like a church. Master Lyons was much stricter than Dominie Siddons had been. Master Lyons used a tawse (a whip with many lashes) to punish both the students who failed to memorize their lessons and those who misbehaved. The boys had many subjects to learn at school. They studied Latin, French, English, arithmetic, spelling, and geography. They also read a great many stories.

In the grammar-school yard, John found that fights were even rougher than they had been at the primary school. Most of the boys expected to become soldiers when they grew up, and they fought and punished one another in the hope of learning to endure harsh treatment.

The boys—and a few of the girls—enjoyed racing up the hill of Davel Brae. John often came in first. One day a girl named Agnes Purns beat him in a race up the hill. John was determined that such a thing would never happen again. He set himself to work running up the hill in the evenings whenever he could get out of the house. His discipline soon made him the best racer among his schoolmates.

Life for the Muir children, however, wasn't all fighting, racing, and school. Life in Dunbar was also full of stories of heroes, ghosts, and monsters. After school and on Saturdays, the boys often ran down to the harbor to play. Some of the stories they heard told of monsters and supernatural creatures called *sookin-in-goats*. The thought of these creatures terrified the boys. Sookin-in-goats were believed to haunt the water and to lurk beneath the surface ready to grab boys who came along. The boys always plunged a stick into the water before they went in, just to be sure that no sookin-in-goat lay in wait for them.

As if this weren't enough, servant girls frightened the children with stories of "Dandy Doctors." *Dandy Doctors* was a term used for real people who sold corpses to medical schools, but that's not what the servants told the boys. The stories the boys heard maintained that Dandy Doctors were men who kidnapped young boys and cut them up for scientific experiments. Dandy Doctors were supposed to wear long black cloaks under which they hid young boys.

One day after school, an older boy saw some strangers in long cloaks. He called out, "A Dandy Doctor! A Dandy Doctor!" and all the boys ran back into the Davel Brae school. The teacher, who was accustomed to seeing them run out of school as soon as they were dismissed, was astonished. The boys were so frightened that they refused to leave until some older boys agreed to walk them to the top of Davel Brae. Then they quickly ran home. That year, no boy was willing to walk home alone after dark.

The countryside around Dunbar was full of natural wonders. The children gathered seashells on the beach and learned to recognize the birds along the shore. But the boys also tormented the birds by shooting at them with home-made guns fashioned out of pipes into which they put real gunpowder. Fortunately for the birds, these makeshift weapons usually caused more fright than real harm.

Most of all, the boys of Dunbar enjoyed *scootchers*. Scootchers were daring stunts, proof of their bravery. In one of these scootchers, John and David dared each other to go into an unused room in their house. This room had a window that had been boarded up because there was a tax on every window. The room still contained the scientific equipment of the doctor who used to live there. John and David believed that the doctor's ghost lived in that room, so they needed great courage to walk inside. John would take a few steps into the room, then run out and dare David to go as far as he had gone.

One of John's most daring scootchers took place at

night. He slipped out of the window in his room and hung from the windowsill, first by two hands, then by one, and finally by just a finger. Before he started out, he asked David to be sure to get their father and a ladder if he couldn't get back in, but that never became necessary. To put the finishing touches on this scootcher, John went out and sat on the peak of the roof, with his nightshirt billowing in the wind. Not wanting to be outdone by his brother, David tried to copy his brother, but terror overcame him, and John had to rescue him.

John and David also joined other boys in scootchers at Dunbar Castle. They climbed the ruins and reenacted some of the battles that had taken place there. John described their adventures many years later.

> We tried to see who could climb highest on the crumbling peaks and crags, and took chances that no cautious mountaineer would try. That I did not fall and finish my rock-scrambling in those adventurous boyhood days seems now a reasonable wonder.

Usually the boys climbed up the castle ruins, but when the tide was out and more land under the castle was exposed, they explored the dungeons below. One day when the tide was out, a group of boys decided to explore the deeper pits below the castle. Only John was daring enough to climb down into the deepest pit of all. He dug his feet and hands into the rock as he slowly lowered himself to the very bottom. It was frightening down there, and he knew that he still had to climb out before the tide came in. He wasn't sure he could get out in time. Neither were his companions.

Above the pit, the other boys called to him, "Are ye doon, Johnny?"

"Aye," said John, slowly inching his way out. Everybody held their breath.

That pit reminded John of the stories he had heard about hell. Later that day, a servant woman scolded him for getting his clothes dirty. She said, "Do you know where bad boys like you go? To hell, that's where they go!"

"Weel, an' I do," replied John. "I'll climb out o' it. I ken I can, because I did!" ["Well, if I do, I'll climb out of it. I know I can because I did!"]

Springtime brought the boys of Dunbar to the fields west of the town. Sometimes they raided the fields for apples, but most of the time they looked for birds and birds' nests. They competed to see who had seen the greatest number of birds' nests. Some birds' nests were considered to be more valuable than others, and that counted, too. Usually they didn't disturb the nests, but sometimes they took baby birds home with them and put them into cages.

In the fields the boys watched the larks soar straight upward into the sky, singing as they ascended. Each boy tried to be the last one to see the lark. They watched, shouting, "I see him yet! I see him yet!" But the lark's song could be heard long after the bird had soared beyond their sight.

The boys sometimes caught a lark and took it home. They put it into a cage, with a sod of grass at the bottom. The poor bird hovered at the top of the cage but couldn't fly high. John once kept a caged lark for a year. Then he released it into the fields, where he watched it soar upward to freedom. This incident was very important to John. Later in life, in his thoughts and writings, wildness and freedom went hand in hand.

Daniel Muir didn't want his sons running wild in the fields with the other boys. He thought their companions would get them into trouble and teach them bad language. Farmers even considered the gangs of boys to be dangerous.

Daniel Muir therefore ordered his sons to stay in the walled-in garden at the back of their house. John always climbed over the wall, dragging David behind him, to escape to the fields. When they returned, their mother often helped them get into bed before their father found out what they had been doing. Whenever he did find out, he gave them a whipping.

Back in school, John found most of his lessons dull, but he loved the stories he read about heroes and other lands. He and his classmates also read about strange plants and animals in America. John was fascinated by tales of the bald eagle and the fish hawk—birds that didn't live in Scotland. He read John Audubon's description of passenger pigeons, which flew in great flocks that darkened the sky. Most of all, John was fascinated by tales of sugar maples—those strange trees that yielded sugar.

In 1848, all of Dunbar talked about the gold that was being discovered in California. America and other countries became part of the boys' bedtime games. After they were supposed to be asleep, John and David would get under the covers and pretend they were traveling to far-off lands. They made up one adventure after another until they were too tired to stay awake. After they had fallen asleep, their mother would go in and gently place their heads on the pillow and tuck the covers around them.

One day John and David were at Grandfather Gilrye's reciting their lessons as usual. Their father came in and said, "Bairns, you needna learn your lessons the nicht, for we're gan to America the morn!" ["Children, you need not learn your lessons tonight, for we're going to America in the morning."]

John Muir called it "the most wonderful, most glorious" news "that wild boys ever heard." He thought, "No more grammar, but boundless woods full of mysterious good things...."

For Grandfather Gilrye, however, the news wasn't happy. He loved the boys and their afternoon visits, and he knew how much he would miss them. He worried that their father would become even stricter far away in America. Grandfather Gilrye also knew that there was a lot of hard work in store for the Muirs in America. He listened to the boys discuss the maple sugar and strange birds, and he worried.

"Ah, poor laddies! Poor laddies!" he said. "You'll find something else ower [over] the sea forbye [besides] gold, and sugar, birds' nests and freedom fra [from] lessons and schools. You'll find plenty hard, hard work."

Grandfather Gilrye gave John and David a gold coin each as a going-away gift.

John and David ran through the streets calling to their friends, "I'm gan to Amaraka the morn!" But none of their friends believed them.

2

"That Glorious Wisconsin Wilderness!"

The next morning, only four members of the Muir family left for America. Daniel Muir and three of the children—thirteen-year-old Sarah, eleven-year-old John, and nine-year-old David—went with him to find a place to settle. He sold the house and the business in Dunbar. In America, he planned to clear land for a farm and to build a new house.

In the meantime, Anne Muir and the four remaining children moved in with her parents. Fifteen-year-old Margaret stayed in Scotland to help her mother take care of the youngest children—Danny and the twin girls, Mary and Annie.

The travelers took a train to Glasgow, Scotland. Daniel Muir hadn't been back to Glasgow since he ran away from his sister's farm. On February 18, 1849, they boarded a sailing ship bound for America.

In those days, passengers on ships cooked their own food. There were rows of stoves on the deck for this purpose.

At home, however, all their meals were cooked at the fireplace. Thirteen-year-old Sarah had never used a stove, and she looked at the rows of stoves in bewilderment. It didn't matter, though, because before long she realized that she was too seasick even to think about food. Poor Sarah was sick during the entire voyage and had to stay below the decks. Her father was almost as miserable.

John and David had no problem with the rolling ship. They enjoyed the voyage, which lasted six weeks and three days. Once their father showed up on deck to give them some candy their mother had sent along, but he felt sick and quickly disappeared again below the decks.

The two boys loved to watch the sailors at work. They learned the names of the ropes and sails. They even tried to help the sailors. The ship's captain was surprised to learn that the two Scottish boys, whose speech had a strong Scottish accent, spoke fluent English as well. He lent them books to read and invited them to join him in his cabin.

When Daniel Muir left Scotland, he had no definite idea where he and his family would settle. At first he thought he might try Canada, but on the ship he heard stories that changed his mind. The land in Canada, people told him, was thickly wooded and would take many years to clear. In the United States, however, the land had more openings among the trees and could be cleared and farmed during the first year. People on the ship spoke of good land that was available in Wisconsin. Daniel didn't have a very clear picture of North American geography. He didn't even know that Wisconsin had just become a state in 1848, but he listened to what people said.

Daniel Muir believed that he was going into an un-civilized land, so he brought many heavy possessions with him. These included scales with heavy weights and many tools that were more out of date than those he could have bought in the United States.

The Muirs landed in New York City and loaded their belongings onto a riverboat that was going up the Hudson River to Albany, New York. At Albany they transferred to a canal boat that traveled the Erie Canal to Buffalo. At Buffalo they had to change to a Great Lakes steamer that would take them through the Great Lakes to Milwaukee, Wisconsin. When they landed, Daniel bought a cast-iron stove and added it to their already heavy belongings.

At Milwaukee, Daniel Muir left his children in a boardinghouse while he went to look for someone who could take them farther west. He hired a driver with a wagon and horses to carry them and their baggage for thirty dollars. He had heard that there was good land near Kingston, in Marquette County. The wagon driver was dismayed when he discovered what a heavy load his horses would have to pull. He regretted that he had promised to take them.

Daniel Muir left his children in a room in Kingston while he went to look for Alexander Gray, a Scotsman who had been recommended as someone who could help him find a homestead—a place to settle. Before the family left Kingston, Daniel bought the children a horse he had promised them, an Indian pony named Jack.

It was ten miles from Kingston to the Grays' house, and the Muirs traveled in a cart pulled by oxen. John was amazed at the beasts and wondered "how the great oxen could be so strong and wise and tame as to pull so heavy a load with no other harness than a chain and a crooked piece of wood on their necks, and how they could sway so obediently to right and left past roadside trees and stumps when the driver said *haw* and *gee*," which meant left and right.

The children stayed with Alexander Gray's family for a

few nights. The boys slept in the barn, and Sarah slept in the bedroom with Mrs. Gray. Mrs. Gray taught Sarah how to use a stove instead of a fireplace for cooking. Then Daniel Muir returned and they set out for their new home.

The first thing John and David saw when they reached their farm was a blue jay's nest. The boys ran wild at the sight of what John called "that glorious Wisconsin wilderness." They saw birds and plants they had never seen before. They discovered a bluebird's nest and then a woodpecker's. They found frogs, snakes, and turtles. They were overjoyed at the beauty of it all. In later years, John described this experience that struck them as so different from the life they had known in Scotland.

Nature streaming into us, wooingly teaching her wonderful glowing lessons, so unlike the dismal grammar ashes and cinders so long thrashed into us. Here without knowing it, we still were at school; every wild lesson a love lesson, not whipped but charmed into us.

With help from several neighbors, Daniel Muir built a shanty in the woods to house the family until they could build a real house. The shanty had wooden floors and one window.

Daniel Muir also hired a Yankee to help with the farm work. The boys soon discovered that the Yankee could answer many of their questions about the new animals and plants around them.

One day John heard a strange drumming noise. He couldn't imagine what it was and decided that his head or stomach must be making the odd sound. He asked David about it. David heard it, too. At last they discovered that it was the beating of the wings of a partridge that was courting its mate.

John asked the Yankee the name of another bird that made a very strange call. "Why, it's telling you its name," answered the Yankee. "Don't you hear it and what he wants you to do? He says his name is 'Poor Will' and he wants you to whip him."

One evening near the farm's lake, John saw strange twinklings of tiny lights in the meadow. He thought "the whole wonderful fairy show" had to be in his eyes because he had never seen anything like it. He asked David if he saw anything.

"Yes," replied David. "It's all covered with shaky fire-sparks."

The two boys asked the Yankee about the strange lights. "Oh, it's nothing but lightnin'-bugs," said the Yankee, and he led them into the meadow to catch a few lightning bugs. The boys carried them into the shanty and watched them twinkle on and off for a while, "as if each little passionate glow were caused by the beating of a heart."

By this time, the children had not only a pony, but a cat and a puppy. When the cat had kittens, the mother began bringing all kinds of small animals to feed them. Some of the birds and animals were creatures that John and David hadn't yet discovered around the farm. The puppy, which they named Watch, began to serve as a watchdog. One day Watch caught a new scent and looked west to its source. The boys followed him to a site overlooking the lake and meadow. There they saw a Native American (American Indian) hunter catching muskrats with a spear.

The local Native Americans had been conquered and forced off their land a few years earlier. Occasionally one or two would come to the door asking for food. Once Sarah was alone in the house when an Indian walked up with a hatchet in his hand. She felt frightened, but the man simply went over to the sharpening stone, sharpened his hatchet, and left.

Daniel Muir once had a discussion with a neighbor about the rightful ownership of the land. The neighbor thought it was unfortunate that the Native Americans had been robbed of their land and forced to lose their livelihood. Daniel Muir's opinion was that God didn't intend to allow the Native Americans to keep the land in an unproductive way when Scottish, Irish, and English farmers could put it to more productive use and spread the Gospel as well. The neighbor replied that if that was so, then other, better farmers could use the same argument to drive the Muirs and their neighbors off the land.

Listening to this discussion, John agreed with the neighbor, but he said nothing. It made him think about how the people in Scotland had been conquered and driven off their land by the English, who thought their way of life was better than the Scottish way.

At first it seemed that Grandfather Gilrye had been wrong about the "hard, hard work." That first summer, the boys had a great deal of freedom while their father and hired workers cleared the land. They cleared it by burning the grass and then uprooting tree stumps. John hated the sight of the great fires and the waste of nature they caused. The boys had to remove the debris, but it wasn't really hard work. John's only regular job was helping Sarah with the laundry every Monday. He and his sister always ended up quarreling before the work was done.

When they weren't helping their father or exploring the land, John and David taught themselves to ride Jack, the pony. They received no lessons but learned by falling off and getting back on again. Within a few months, both boys had mastered the horse. But soon both Watch and Jack would be taken from them. When Watch was about six or seven, the neighbors accused the dog of eating their chickens. John and David couldn't believe that their beloved dog would "do anything so grossly undoglike." Their father listened to the neighbors and shot Watch. Then he examined the dog's stomach. Sure enough, he found the remains of chickens the dog had eaten. "So poor Watch was killed," John later said, "simply because his taste for chickens was too much like our own."

Jack's fate was different. The boys often used their pony to round up the cows. Sometimes the horse went after the cows on its own. Daniel Muir thought the horse behaved too much like a sheepdog, and he ordered John to shoot Jack. Somehow Jack's life was spared, but he was sold shortly afterward to someone who was going to California.

The children helped build a frame house that the entire family could live in. Daniel bought good lumber from Milwaukee, and carpenters were hired to do much of the work. The workers called it "a palace of a house." When it was finished, the Muir house had eight rooms and was two and a half stories high. For many years, it enjoyed the reputation of being the finest house in the area. Sarah made curtains and decorated the new home with flowers as her mother would have done. The family planted flowers in front of the house.

In November, Daniel rode into Milwaukee to meet his wife and Margaret, Danny, and the twins (who had turned three on the voyage from Scotland). They reached the farm on November 7, 1849. Now, after being apart for almost a year, the family would be together again. One more child would eventually join them. Joanna, the youngest, was the parents' only child to be born in America.

Even though the next day was a Sunday and Daniel Muir usually didn't allow strolling on the Sabbath, he proudly walked the newcomers around their new home. Daniel Muir named his farm Fountain Lake Farm because many springs flowed down the hills into the lake.

By December the snows were deep, and the family was cut off from the outside world. They dug tunnels through the snow and traveled beneath the white frozen world to get from one place to another within the farm.

Spring brought many changes. John's days of freedom were soon over. He faced the beginning of many years of brutally hard work. He wrote:

> I was put to the plough [plow] at the age of twelve, when my head reached but a little above the handles, and for many years I had to do the greater part of the ploughing.

Yet plowing was a challenge, and John took pride in doing it well. He often tried to outdo the hired men. He boasted, "None could draw a straighter furrow." He soon discovered that his work would be easier if he kept his tools sharp and in good order. Besides plowing, John split rails to make snake, or zigzag, fences. His father supervised them but did little of the farm work. He insisted that the oldest children—John, Margaret, Sarah, David, and eventually Danny—spend long hours laboring in the fields. The work was so hard that it affected the children's health for the rest of their lives.

John and Margaret formed a team for reaping the wheat. John used a large tool called a cradle to cut the wheat, and Margaret followed after to gather and bundle it. Margaret could bundle six acres of grain a day. Most men could bundle only three. When the time came for hoeing, each child was assigned a different row so they wouldn't waste time talking to one another.

Even though they lived on a farm, the Muir children were often sick from lack of good food. To make matters worse, they had no medical care. Once John came down with pneumonia after his father sent him out into a storm to find a missing sheep. Daniel Muir refused to send for a doctor because he believed that prayer was all that was needed to heal his children's illnesses. As soon as John was able to stand on his feet, before he was fully recovered from the pneumonia, he was sent back to the fields to do more plowing.

Many of the Muirs' neighbors belonged to the Disciples of Christ. Many Campbellites had become Disciples of Christ and believed that Jesus' Second Coming was going to happen soon. This was the religious group to which Daniel Muir belonged. This sect believed in lay preachers rather than formally trained ministers, and Daniel Muir began to gain a reputation as a good preacher. As time went on, he spent more and more of his time preaching. One of the neighbors who disapproved of the way Muir worked his children commented, "He preferred preaching to working."

Many of the Muirs' neighbors had also come from Scotland. Philip Gray was a member of the same religious group as the Muirs. He had two sons, David and John who became friends of John and David Muir.

Another new settler was the young and handsome David Galloway, who had come to America to find land for his parents and sisters. Although he was older than John Muir, the two became friends. They quoted the Scottish poet Robert Burns to each other and sang together.

It soon became clear that David Galloway was in love with Sarah Muir and she with him. But they couldn't think of marriage yet. First he needed to clear land and start a farm. Then he had to return to Scotland to bring his parents and the rest of his family to Wisconsin.

Meanwhile, Daniel Muir bought more and more land. The new land, which the family called Hickory Hill, was six miles from Fountain Lake Farm. Although he protested, John was put to work clearing the land at Hickory Hill while Margaret and Sarah worked at Fountain Lake. By now, Danny and the twins were also being made to work at farming.

When David Galloway returned from Scotland with his family, he saw how thin and pale Sarah was and he worried about her. He and Sarah lost no time making plans to get married.

David Galloway and Daniel Muir arranged a land exchange so that neither would have parcels of scattered land. As part of the arrangement, David Galloway gave his own eighty acres next to Hickory Hill to the Muirs, and he received the Muirs' original eighty-acre section. As a result of the exchange, the Galloways had land that John Muir had already cleared for his father, and the Muirs had land that still needed to be cleared.

In December 1856, Sarah Muir and David Galloway were married. From that time on, Sarah no longer worked in the fields. Yet the labor her father had forced upon her made her a partial invalid for much of her life.

John Muir was particularly fond of Mrs. Galloway, David's mother, and she befriended him. She was very impressed with this young boy, and she predicted that he would go far. She was the first to give him the encouragement he needed.

During the autumn of 1854, John Muir, along with some other young men, was selected to work on a community project. They had to build a corduroy road across a swamp. A corduroy road is a road built of logs laid side by side. Among the others who had been selected were David Gray and David Taylor. The two Davids, known as the "Twa Davies," had a great deal in common. They both loved reading and poetry. As they worked (John did most of the work), the Twa Davies recited poetry. John had never heard poetry recited so beautifully. He went home that night "anxious to know all the poets," and from that day on he began saving his money to buy books. He also began to borrow books from neighbors. But these books led to conflicts with his father, who believed that the Bible was the only book anyone needed to read.

Daniel Muir thought that novels were especially evil. One day he caught John with a copy of a novel by Sir Walter Scott, and he was furious. He forbade his son to read such books. John soon learned to hide any books he thought his father would disapprove of. His mother, sisters, and brothers all helped John in this.

Whenever Daniel Muir was away, the family enjoyed activities he didn't permit. Anne Muir taught her daughters to embroider and to make lace. John often read aloud to them while they worked. By this time, Mrs. Muir was able to buy pretty dresses and ribbons for her girls and fine linen to make shirts for her boys. Her father had changed his will when Daniel Muir left for America. Grandfather Gilrye didn't want Daniel Muir to have control of Anne Muir's money. When her father died in 1852, Anne Muir began to receive money for herself four times a year. She used this money as she chose.

John managed to persuade his father to buy him an arithmetic book, but he had to promise that the farm work wouldn't suffer. Within a single summer, John taught him-

This photograph of John Muir's mother, Anne Gilrye Muir, was taken at Portage, Wisconsin, in 1863.

self higher arithmetic by studying daily between midday dinner and the time the workers went out to the fields for the afternoon. He then taught himself algebra, geometry, and trigonometry.

Daniel Muir was willing to buy his son a few religious books but little else. Once when John borrowed a book called *Christian Philosopher*, his father became angry. He objected to the word *philosopher*.

John soon realized that to win an argument with his father, he would have to quote the Bible. When his father placed the entire family on a diet of vegetables and graham flour, his mother continued to put meat on the table. Naturally Daniel Muir objected. John came to her rescue by quoting the story of the Prophet Elijah. The Lord had sent ravens to Elijah, and the birds fed Elijah with flesh. His father admitted that he was mistaken. If the Lord had provided meat for Elijah, then meat was acceptable as food.

John's appetite for books was growing, and he wanted to attend school. For a short period of two months, he was allowed to go to the district school. The school was also the center of teenage social life, including spelling bees. One day John Muir and Katie Cairns were the last two students left in a spelling bee. The two spelled word after word correctly. Finally there was one that John missed, and Katie won.

"Katie, ye'll never spell me doon again!" declared John. After that, he spent many hours studying spelling, and Katie never again beat him.

John's brother David liked Katie, and he began to comb his hair and dress more carefully. John, however, showed no interest in any of the local girls.

Farming Hickory Hill meant there was more land to clear and more backbreaking work for the children—especially John. Their father woke them early every morning

25

and rarely gave them time off during the day. He decided what time the entire family would go to bed at night, and no one was allowed to stay up beyond that time. The only room in which he permitted a fire was the kitchen. When the children awoke on cold winter mornings, they had to put their feet on cold floors and into frozen boots. They couldn't get warm until the kitchen fire was blazing.

Even worse, Hickory Hill Farm had no source of water. It needed a well. William Duncan, a neighbor, suggested that the Muirs use dynamite to blast the sandstone rock, but Daniel Muir insisted that John use a chisel to carve out the rock to dig the well. Day after day, John climbed into a bucket and was lowered into the well, where he chipped away by the light of a candle. When the well was about eighty feet deep, John was lowered to the bottom one morning and was overcome by faintness. His father heard no sounds coming from the bottom. John came close to death.

"What's keeping you so still?" called his father.

John could barely answer. "Take me out!" he cried in a feeble voice.

When Daniel Muir began hoisting the bucket, he discovered that it was too light. John wasn't in it.

"Get in! Get in the bucket and hold on! Hold on!" he shouted.

John somehow managed to get into the bucket and was dragged out gasping for breath.

Their neighbor William Duncan heard about the accident and came by to see how John was. He explained that there was such a thing as chokedamp—poisonous gases that settle at the bottom of a well. He showed the Muirs how to throw water down the well shaft to absorb the gas and to use hay attached to a rope to carry pure air down and to stir up and get rid of the poisonous gases.

Within a day or two, Daniel Muir again lowered John into the well shaft. John dug ten more feet until at last he struck water.

Describing this experience, John later said:

Constant dropping wears away stone. So does constant chipping, while at the same time wearing away the chipper. Father never spent an hour in that well. He trusted me to sink it straight and plumb, and I did, and built a fine covered top over it, and swung two iron-bound buckets in it from which we all drank for many a day.

William Duncan became a friend of John's and encouraged the boy to develop his mind and his talents. As John went about the farm, he often whittled things out of wood. His father, too, had whittled as a young man, but he now thought this was a worthless way to spend time.

John desperately wanted more time for his reading. One evening after family worship, he tried to stay up later than the family bedtime. But his father ordered him to bed, saying that John had to go to bed when everybody else did.

"If you *will* read," added Daniel Muir, "get up in the morning and read. You may get up in the morning as early as you like."

John went to bed that night hoping that he would awaken before his father called him. When he awoke early, he ran downstairs and held a candle to the kitchen clock. It was one o'clock. He was delighted.

"Five hours to myself!" he thought. "Five huge, solid hours!"

It was too cold to read, though, and John knew that his father would object to his making a fire no matter how cold it was. His "father might object to the cost of firewood that took time to chop."

Instead of reading, John went down to the cellar, which was below his father's room. He began working on a model of a self-setting sawmill he had invented. Morning after morning, he awoke early and went to the freezing cellar to work on his invention by candlelight. He discovered that of the tools his father had brought from Scotland, very few were useful. John needed a fine-toothed saw, so he made one out of a steel stay from a corset. He made other tools he needed as well.

The noise in the cellar probably disturbed Daniel Muir's sleep, but he was a man of his word and would not go back on the permission he had given. After a few weeks of this, however, he could no longer stand it. At the breakfast table one morning, he decided to bring up the subject.

"John," he asked, "what time is it when you get up in the morning?"

"About one o'clock," John replied.

"And what kind of time is that, getting up in the middle of the night and disturbing the whole family?" he demanded.

John simply reminded his father that he had given his permission.

"I *know* it," his father responded. "I *know* I gave you that miserable permission, but I never imagined that you would get up in the middle of the night."

John continued to work on the sawmill. When it was finished, he tried it out in a stream in the meadow, and it worked. He designed several other inventions—including a waterwheel, locks and latches for doors, a thermometer, a barometer, and many kinds of clocks. He whittled the small pieces of the clocks as he went about the farm. He also made timing machines. He hid one of these in a spare room upstairs, and his father discovered it.

"John," Margaret whispered to him, "Fayther [father] saw that thing you're making upstairs."

John was worried. His father asked him what he was making, and John said he didn't know what to call it.

"What!" exclaimed his father. "You mean to say you don't know what you are trying to do?"

John answered that he did know what it was for, but he didn't know what to call it. It was for getting people up in the morning, he told his father. He decided to call it an early-rising machine.

John made another clock that was shaped like a scythe. On the scythe's handle he wrote, "All flesh is grass." This biblical quotation pleased his father. He made another clock with four dials facing four different directions. John wanted to place this clock on the roof of the barn so that people could tell the time while they worked in the fields, but his father objected. He didn't want crowds of people coming to the barn to look at it. John also invented a huge thermometer that was so sensitive that the dial would move as people approached it.

Soon people in the neighborhood began to talk about John Muir and his inventions. Some thought he was an oddball. Others, like William Duncan, thought he was a genius. By now, John was twenty-one. He was legally an adult and could leave the farm if he wanted to. But as unhappy as he was, he didn't know where else he would go.

During the summer of 1860, William Duncan stopped by the Muir farm. He had just read that there would be a State Agricultural Fair in Madison, the capital of Wisconsin.

Duncan told John that all he had to do was exhibit his inventions, and people with machine shops would offer him jobs.

John didn't think so. After all, he said, his inventions were just made of wood.

"Made of wood! Made of wood!" exclaimed Duncan. "What does it matter what they're made of when they are so out-and-out original. There's nothing else like them in the world."

John was encouraged. He prepared to take a few inventions to the fair.

Daniel Muir had often warned his children that even though he was hard on them, strangers would be much harder. But John soon discovered that this wasn't so. Strangers often offered him more kindness and sympathy than his father had ever shown.

When John told his father that he was going to the fair, he asked if his father would send him money if he needed it.

"No," said Daniel Muir, "depend entirely on yourself."

3

Inventor and College Student

John left Hickory Hill Farm to try his fortune at the state capital. With him he took several of his inventions—a thermometer, two clocks, and the mechanism for an early-rising machine. He had about fifteen dollars in his pocket. This included the gold coin that Grandfather Gilrye had given him when he left Scotland, a gold coin his mother gave him when he left the farm, and a few dollars he himself had earned by working on other farms. His father gave him nothing.

David drove his brother to the train station at Pardeeville in a wagon. There the young inventor and his strange package attracted attention. On the train John made friends with the conductor and asked if he could ride to Madison with the engineer. His curiosity about the workings of the train led him from one part of the locomotive to another. First he rode in the cab of the engine, then he stood outside on the footboard to observe how the pistons worked.

Finally he sat on the cowcatcher in the front of the train.

At the fairgrounds John learned that people who had inventions to exhibit didn't have to pay an admission charge. The gatekeeper directed him to the Temple of Art, where the inventions were on display.

With the help of a carpenter who had been assigned to him, John built shelves for the clocks and a bed to which he would attach the early-rising machine. Two small boys wandered in and were fascinated by what they saw. This gave John an idea. He asked the boys' parents if he could use them to demonstrate the early-rising machine.

The boys were overjoyed. As spectators looked on, they pretended to be asleep in the bed. At each "wake-up time," the bed tipped at an angle and the boys tumbled out. It was

John Muir's drawing of his early-rising machine. This invention tipped the sleeper out of bed at wake-up time.

great fun! John didn't know it, but these two boys were the sons of two professors at the University of Wisconsin at Madison. One was the son of Professor Ezra Slocum Carr, whose wife, Jeanne Carr, was in charge of the Temple of Art. The other boy was the son of Professor James Davie Butler.

The fair opened. The next day, John Muir's inventions were featured on the front page of the local newspaper. On the fair's second and third days, large crowds poured in to see the clocks, the thermometer with a dial that showed a higher temperature as people drew near, and most of all, the early-rising machine.

John had always been a good talker, and he knew how to draw a crowd of people and hold their attention. In demonstrating the early-rising machine, he would set the mechanism attached to the bed two or three minutes ahead. Then he talked about his other inventions. While the crowd stood listening, the mechanism ticked away and before long made the bed tip at the scheduled time. His exhibits were a great success.

There was only one other invention at the fair that attracted as much attention as John's early-rising machine. It was the *Lady Franklin*, an iceboat invented by Norman Wiard. Wiard assured the audience that the iceboat could travel across frozen water.

When the fair closed, Mrs. Carr's committee awarded John fifteen dollars for his inventions. He also received several job offers, but it was the iceboat that really fascinated him. He thought the inventor was a genius. When Norman Wiard offered to teach John mechanical drawing in exchange for his help in making adjustments on the iceboat, John was excited. He wouldn't get paid for his work, but he expected to learn a great deal.

John Muir and Norman Wiard loaded the iceboat onto

a train heading for the town of Prairie du Chien, where Wiard had a workshop. Because he would receive no salary, John had to find work to support himself. He found two jobs—taking care of a cow and a horse and doing chores at the Mondell Hotel, which was run by the Pelton family. The Peltons had a son named Willie and a very sickly baby named Fanny. They also had a niece, named Emily Pelton, who befriended John and introduced him to her friends.

John grew fond of the Pelton family—especially little Fanny. He liked to soothe her when she cried by singing songs and talking softly.

While John was in Prairie du Chien, his father had softened toward him. At his wife's urging, Daniel Muir sent his son a store-bought suit because he realized that John was out in the world and needed to look his best.

John, however, was not prepared for life in Prairie du Chien. Probably because he had never had much time for fun and games, he was shocked at some of the things Emily and her friends did for amusement. For example, they played kissing games. John wrote home expressing shock at their behavior. David and Sarah Galloway worried that John might become a prude if he didn't learn how to have fun. In fact, David Galloway made a special trip to Prairie du Chien to talk to John and explain how young people behaved. He told John that Emily and her friends weren't misbehaving, that they were simply having a good time. Galloway was pretty sure that John and Emily would eventually get married, but he was wrong. Emily remained a friend, and she and John wrote to each other for many years.

Meanwhile, the *Lady Franklin* kept breaking down. An iceboat was a good idea, but Norman Wiard didn't have enough scientific knowledge to make it work. He tried it out once, and when it failed, he and John made some improvements. But the iceboat failed again the second time. When it failed for the third time, the townspeople became angry at the inventor, who had raised their hopes for winter travel over the frozen waterways.

John himself was annoyed with Wiard for another reason. John had agreed to work on the iceboat in return for lessons, but Wiard had given him only one lesson and had expected him to do a lot of work. John decided that he had no reason to remain in Prairie du Chien, and he returned to Madison.

For John, the real attraction of Madison was the university. He was painfully aware that he had never finished grammar school, but he wished there was some way that he could study at the university. He found work in the capital, and whenever he could, he went over to the university and walked around the buildings.

One day John met a student who remembered his inventions from the state fair. He thought John was attending the university, and John had to explain that he had neither the schooling nor the money that he needed to attend. The student told him there were cheap ways to eat and the school itself didn't charge a high fee. John soon learned that attending the university wasn't as expensive as he thought. Tuition and fees were thirty-two dollars. Many students found that they could scrape by on only fifty cents a week for food.

Although he was still uncertain about his chances of being accepted as a student, John went to have a talk with Dean John Stirling. John was sure that he would be turned down. After all, except for the Dunbar Grammar School back in Scotland and two months of school in Wisconsin, he had taught himself most of what he knew. But to his delight, the dean said that although he would have to spend a few weeks taking a preparatory course, he would be permitted to enter the university as a student. To John, this was like being let into the Kingdom of Heaven.

During his first year, John studied chemistry and geology (the study of the earth by examining its rocks) with Dr. Ezra Slocum Carr, the father of one of the boys who had helped him demonstrate his early-rising machine. He also studied Greek and Latin with Dr. James Davie Butler, the father of the other boy. John was surprised to learn that he still remembered much of his grammar-school Latin. This combination of courses didn't lead to a degree, however, so John Muir was listed as an "Irregular Gent."

Before long, most of the students on the campus knew about John Muir. The thump of his early-rising machine could be heard in his dormitory as he awoke each morning. He also invented a desk to help him schedule his study time. The desk was attached to a timer. Each book to be studied was lifted to its place for a specific amount of time. When the time for studying that subject was up, the desk closed that book and brought up another. Other students came to stare at John's strange inventions.

The young Carr boy was also fascinated. He insisted that his mother come and look at the many wonderful inventions in John Muir's room. Jeanne Carr saw one invention that interested her more than any other. It was a device for measuring a plant's growth. Mrs. Carr was a botanist (someone who studies plants).

Dr. and Mrs. Carr were so impressed with John's inventions that they invited him to their home. They encouraged him to use their library, which was better than the one at the university. Dr. Carr was up on the latest scientific developments. He had also studied the work of the Swiss scientist Louis Agassiz, whose writings John soon found

John Muir's drawing for his desk. Muir's fellow college students were amazed by this invention. A timer could close up a textbook and bring up another and open it after the allotted time for studying the first book was over.

himself poring over with eager curiosity. Agassiz had a new theory about glaciers—huge thick sheets of slow-moving ice. According to Agassiz, during one of the great ice ages, glaciers had carved and changed the shape of the land. In his writings Agassiz described how students of geology could tell that a particular area of land had been shaped by glaciers. These descriptions were written in French, but that didn't stop John. He had been forced to study French in grammar school, so he had little difficulty reading what Agassiz had written.

Professor Carr also pursued another of Agassiz's ideas. Until that time, science was taught mainly in lectures. But Agassiz believed that students of geology should go out and examine the land. It was Agassiz who had said, "Study nature not books." Professor Carr may have been one of the first professors to teach his students about natural science by taking them on field trips.

In April 1861, the Civil War broke out. At the time, the war seemed very far from John Muir and the university. He disliked wars and believed that many people died needlessly.

When school ended that year, John walked all the way home for his vacation. His sister Margaret was no longer living at Hickory Hill Farm. She had married and was now Mrs. John Reid. That summer Daniel Muir paid John seventy-five cents a day to work on the farm. John saved his money for the coming school year. He also helped his brother David learn enough science to join him at the university in the autumn.

At the end of the summer, the brothers left for the university with almost seventy-five dollars each for their schooling. It was enough to get them through the fall term, but they would need more money to continue their education. Fortunately, many schools wanted university students as teachers, so John and David soon found jobs teaching at two different schools. John earned twenty dollars a month. He had to leave Madison and the university, but he kept up his studies by reading and corresponding with his teachers. He also visited the university on weekends whenever he could.

John enjoyed teaching, and his students loved him. He didn't have to whip them to make them learn because his own enthusiasm was contagious. It soon spread to other people in the neighborhood. Before long he was being asked to give lectures about science to adults.

The young teacher did not like to walk into an unheated classroom each morning, so he decided to do something to eliminate that problem. He invented a device that would light a fire before classes began. Each afternoon before he left school, he set up a contraption made of ashes, a string, and a timer to light a fire the next morning. Now the school would be warm when he and his students arrived. Although a neighboring farmer worried that John would set fire to the school, the "clock-fire" never failed that winter, and the room was always inviting.

David, on the other hand, found university work too difficult. His only desire was to earn a good living and marry Katie Cairns, the girl who had beaten John in the spelling bee. After teaching for a while, David found a job in Portage working in a store. In time he became a partner in the business.

By March 1862, John was back at Madison. The city had changed a great deal because of the war. There were soldiers everywhere, and with them came a lot of noise, dirt, and cheap hotels and restaurants.

There was also news from home. John's brother Danny had been asking if he, too, could go to school. His father had originally said no, but he later changed his mind. In the end, Daniel Muir decided to rent Hickory Hill Farm to Margaret and John Reid. He then moved his family to Portage, where all the children who were still at home could go to school. Danny, however, was restless. He decided to go to Canada. There had been talk of a military draft. That possibility may have spurred his decision to go to Canada.

At school that year, John happened to meet a student named Griswold, who was interested in botany. Griswold showed him a flower from a locust tree and asked what family John thought the tree belonged to.

"I don't know anything about botany," John replied.

"Well, no matter," Griswold challenged him, "What is it like?"

"It's like a pea flower," John suggested.

Griswold told him he was right, but John didn't understand how a big tree and a weak pea plant could be related. Griswold explained that if you study the parts of the flowers and the plants' seeds, you can see how plants are related. He also told John to taste the locust leaf. It tasted like a pea leaf. Fascinated by what he was learning from Griswold, John went about collecting plants and studying them. Botany would become another of John's lifelong interests.

At school Professor Butler encouraged John to write naturally instead of trying to use formal language. He also urged John to keep a journal. John would be grateful for this advice later in his life.

John's visits to the Carr home continued. The Carrs had lived in Massachusetts before moving to Wisconsin. They were friends of Ralph Waldo Emerson, the great poet and essay writer. They liked to read the works of Emerson and Henry David Thoreau to John. But one of John Muir's favorite writers was Alexander von Humboldt. Humboldt

John Muir was about twenty-five when this photograph of him was taken in Madison, Wisconsin.

had explored large areas of South America and had written books about his journeys.

By 1863, John had enough money to complete his education. His father had given him eighty acres of Hickory Hill. John sold the land for $650, which the farmer was to pay him in small amounts.

One of the people John met that year was a man named Increase Lapham, who warned that it was dangerous for people to be destroying trees as rapidly as they did. Lapham was the first person John Muir had every heard speak about the importance of conservation—saving land and natural resources for future use.

Meanwhile, the Civil War was making Madison a depressing place. Confederate prisoners who had been brought to the city were dying from lack of food and medical care. John couldn't bear to see them suffering. He thought about becoming a medical doctor, and Dr. Carr advised him to go to Ann Arbor, Michigan, to study medicine.

In May 1863, the North began drafting soldiers for the war. John didn't know whether he would be drafted, so he decided this would be a good time to visit friends. The first place he went to was Prairie du Chien to see Emily Pelton. They had continued writing to each other after John left. The two friends had a long walk and talk, but when John went back to see her, her uncle said she was not in. That happened again the next time John called, so he visited Fountain Lake.

He returned to Madison to learn that he had not been drafted. But because of the war, the mail service was so poor that John never received the letter telling him that he had received a fellowship to the university. Like Danny, he was beginning to feel restless. To add to his problems, the man who had bought his land had been unable to keep up the payments. The Muir family wanted John to settle down like his brother David, who had now married Katie Cairns and had a home in Portage.

When it looked as if the war might be coming to an end, John decided to go to Canada. He left in March 1864.

4

On His Own

At this time, John's main interest was botany. He happily wandered through Canada's wet bogs studying one plant after another, but he was looking for one flower in particular—a rare orchid called the Hider of the North.

He traveled light, carrying only his notebook, a compass, and small amounts of tea and oatmeal. Whenever he could, he bought large loaves of bread from the women on the farms he passed. At other times he made himself oatmeal and added the berries, seeds, flowers, and leaves of edible plants. At night he sometimes camped out in the woods. At other times farmers allowed him to sleep in their barns or homes. He also slept in trees in the woods.

John did have a small amount of money with him. But whenever it ran low, he took temporary jobs until he had enough to continue his travels. He was lonely at times, but he enjoyed his nature studies. One day when thoroughly exhausted, John looked for a tree in which he could make a bed for the night. Suddenly something—a tiny shape—caught his eye. It was the Hider of the North. The sight of that flower renewed his spirits and gave him the energy to go on.

Back in the United States, the Civil War was almost over, but Anne Muir still worried that her sons might be drafted. She knew that many young men from Wisconsin had lost their lives or health in the brutal fighting that had now been going on for four years. There would soon be another draft, and she didn't want her sons to be called. She wrote a letter to John asking him to keep his brother Danny from leaving Canada.

John and Danny met at Niagara Falls. Danny told his brother about a job he once had at a sawmill in Trout Hollow. He suggested that they both go there to see if they could find work. When the Muir brothers arrived at the sawmill, the owners were glad to see them. They liked Danny and offered him his old job back at the sawmill.

The company, called Trout and Jay, also had a factory that made wooden tools. When the owners learned that John Muir was an inventor and a mechanic, they offered him a job. They agreed to pay him ten dollars a month plus his room and meals. In addition, he could take time off for botanizing. John gladly accepted the offer. William Trout and Charles Jay, the partners who owned the mill, were a likable pair. But more important to John was the location of the Trout and Jay factory—on the Big Head River right in the midst of some of the most wonderful forests. It was a botanist's heaven.

William Trout was an expert with machines, but he soon realized that John was even better. John figured out how to produce twice as many wooden rakes as before in the same amount of time and using the same number of workers.

William Trout was impressed.

Harriet Trout, one of William's sisters, taught school nearby. She realized that John knew a great deal and asked him to teach Sunday school. Instead of teaching Bible stories, John taught the children science. He quickly gained a reputation for knowing science and explaining it well. Soon adults as well as children began to come to him to learn more about science.

People liked John because of the way he spoke to them and because he was always thoughtful. If the mill workers were out late at night, for example, he left a candle in the window. On chilly nights, he left a warm fire so they wouldn't come home to a cold house.

In the summer of 1865, Jeanne Carr, the wife of John's former professor, began to write letters asking John to exchange ideas with her. John was glad to be back in touch with an old friend. He wrote to her that he was able to read more of God's power and goodness from nature than he had found in the Bible. They soon began a lifelong correspondence. Their letters were mostly about botany, which John found endlessly fascinating. Each morning he set his early-rising machine for five o'clock so that he could go into the woods before going to the factory.

When Trout and Jay received a large order for 30,000 broom handles and 12,000 wooden rakes, the partners asked John to design new equipment. They wanted to increase the factory's output so they could complete the order. If John could produce the rakes and handles on time, the partners promised, they would give him half the profits.

John worked at improving the self-feeding lathe that William Trout had designed. As a result of these improvements, the factory could turn out eight handles a minute instead of four. He then worked at designing machines to make the various parts of the rake itself. Soon all the broom handles and half the rakes were finished. These were stored at the mill so that the wood would be seasoned before the shipment was sent.

That night it was cold and stormy. The Trout family had a roaring fire going in their fireplace. Sparks blew out of the chimney and landed on the roof of the mill. Before anyone could stop it, the fire had destroyed everything.

Trout and Jay were wiped out, but John Muir had done his job and they felt that he should be paid. They had no money at the time. They gave him an IOU in which they offered to pay him $300 as soon as they could. John insisted that it was too much and took an IOU for $200 instead.

John managed to get a little money together and headed back into the United States. When he reached Indianapolis, Indiana, he stopped there because there were so many beautiful forests nearby. In almost no time he found a job with Osgood, Smith & Company, which made carriages. (Automobiles hadn't been invented yet.) The company started John out at ten dollars a week. But before the week was out, the owners saw how good he was and raised his salary to eighteen dollars a week.

John Muir could never leave machines alone when he saw a way to make them more efficient. He designed a machine that made the entire carriage wheel automatically—except for the metal rim, which had to be placed around the wheel by hand. From that time on, his machine became the model for making wagon wheels throughout the country.

Unfortunately, John Muir never patented his ideas. To *patent* means to register an idea and design with the government. A patent is a government document giving the inventor rights to the invention for a limited time. A patent gives the inventor the right to prevent others from making, using, or selling the invention without permission. But John Muir believed that inventions were inspired by God and belonged to everyone. If he had patented his wheel-making machine, the money earned from that single invention would have allowed him to live comfortably for the rest of his life.

Professor Butler, who had kept in touch with John, wrote to ask him to visit a professor he knew who lived in Indianapolis. Catherine Merrill was the second woman professor in the country. She was head of the English department at Butler University. John was shy about visiting a stranger, but he took the letter of introduction Professor Butler had written and went off to see Catherine Merrill.

John was nervously walking back and forth in front of Professor Merrill's house when ten-year-old Merrill Moores, Catherine Merrill's nephew, happened to come out. John timidly showed the young boy the letter, and they went inside.

Years later, Merrill Moores described his first impression of John Muir. He said Muir was "a tall, sturdy man with blue eyes and a clear ruddy complexion as well as handsome hair and beard." He went on to say that John had "a marked Scotch accent and was obviously a working man, but was plainly and neatly dressed; and he at once impressed me as the handsomest man I had ever met."

Catherine Merrill and her sister were delighted to meet the young stranger even though he was dressed as a workman. (Muir never dressed to impress people.) Before long they found themselves listening to and enjoying his stories. He told them about his inventions and about his love of nature. When he left, he promised to visit the sisters again.

The sisters invited John to meet their friends one Sunday afternoon, but when he joined them, he felt as if he were on display. Later visits, however, were spent in the fields, where John felt more at ease. In his element now, he was master of himself as he showed the sisters and their friends a scientific appreciation of the woods.

Soon John was again enlisted to teach Sunday school. As before, nature was his bible. This time his students were the boys of working families. The boys, who adored their enthusiastic teacher, couldn't get enough of his scientific talks and field trips.

John also kept busy with his work at Osgood, Smith & Company. After improving the company's production by inventing his wagon-wheel machine, he began to look at other ways to increase production. In studying the way the factory was set up, he suggested that workers should work only an eight-hour day. He was able to prove that in the extra two hours of their ten-hour day, the workers' efficiency dropped a great deal. Those two hours were almost wasted time, he said.

The factory owners, Mr. Osgood and Mr. Smith, already considered themselves advanced because their workers worked only ten hours, while workers elsewhere put in much longer days. As a result, John's suggestion that they reduce the workday even more seemed too much. Nevertheless, they allowed him to rearrange most of the factory according to his own ideas.

Osgood and Smith liked John because he improved production and was easy to work with. The workers liked him, too. He encouraged them to do their best without threats or punishment. He also listened to their complaints and tried to help them solve some of their problems. Once a worker named Henry Riley thought he might like to try farming instead of factory work. John lent him money to buy land. When Riley didn't succeed at farming, John took him back at the factory and taught him a great deal about machines. Riley became good at his work and never forgot John's generosity.

From his farm days, John Muir knew that machines operate at their best when they're kept in good repair. He often worked at the factory until late into the night. There was no electricity in those days, and most machines were powered by water or steam. Energy was transferred by a series of machine belts.

One afternoon in March, John sat at a workbench repairing a belt while Riley worked nearby. John was using a small file to repair the belt when it suddenly leapt out of his hand and into his right eye. He cupped his hand over his eye. When he removed it, he found that the world had gone dark.

"My right eye gone!" exclaimed John. "Closed forever on all God's beauty!"

Henry Riley led him back to the house where he lived, and the people called their doctor. The doctor told John that he had lost the use of his eye. From the shock of the accident, he was also unable to see out of the left eye. He despaired of ever seeing again and wrote to tell his friends and family.

Professor Catherine Merrill heard about the accident and came to see John. Then she sent for an eye specialist who examined John and assured him that he would be able to see again if he simply rested his eyes in a dark room. Although John still couldn't see, these words of hope made the world seem bright again.

John found many things to do while he was recovering, such as whittling toys for the children of the family in whose house he lived. Often the boys from his Sunday school class came to read to him. Merrill Moores visited regularly to read and to bring flowers. In return, John told the children stories of things he had seen and heard. Many years later, one of those children said that they "cherished the memory of that dark room and of those beautiful stories."

Mr. Osgood and Mr. Smith also visited John every day. They told him they had adopted many of his ideas for setting up the factory. They also offered him the job of foreman of the factory with a higher pay when he recovered. Later, they promised, they would make him a partner.

John told them that he wanted to get outside to the world of nature at least once before giving them an answer. He knew that he was an excellent machinist and inventor. He was also an excellent industrial engineer (someone who sets up a workplace to make it operate efficiently). He could make a good living at this work and help many workers as well. But his heart was in the wilderness. He felt strongly that if he worked with machines much longer, he would never get to do what he really wanted to do.

Although John's eye injury healed, he never recovered completely normal vision in his right eye. About a month after his injury, John went out into the woods. When he came back, he had no doubts about what he wanted to do.

"God has to nearly kill us sometimes, to teach us lessons," he wrote.

He quit his job at Osgood, Smith & Company and went home to Wisconsin. First he stayed with Sarah and David Galloway. Then he went to Hickory Hill Farm, where his family had returned. Merrill Moores went along with him.

At home John and his father argued constantly because Daniel Muir thought botany and geology were evil. He scolded his son for not having a regular job and a family. Then he accused John of "walking in the paths of the Deevil."

"I'll tell you this, Father," John answered. "I've been spending my time a lot nearer the Almighty than you have!"

As John was leaving Hickory Hill, his father asked him if he hadn't forgotten something. John asked what he had forgotten.

"Hae ye no [Haven't you] forgotten to pay for your board [meals] and lodging?" replied Daniel Muir.

John gave his father the money and told him, "Father, you asked me to come home for a visit. I thought I was welcome. You may be very sure it will be a long time before I come again."

John then went on a camping trip with Merrill Moores. They built a raft and floated down the Wisconsin River to Portage, where David Muir lived. David and John talked things over. John had been helping to send his younger sisters and brothers to school, but they no longer needed his help. He therefore decided to treat himself to three years of botanizing.

John Muir was twenty-nine years old and had no responsibilities. He returned to Indianapolis to get his things and to drop off Merrill Moores. Then he set off hoping to be "another Humboldt." On the first page of his journal he wrote, "John Muir—Earth-planet —Universe."

First he crossed into Kentucky and visited the famous Horse Caves. Then he crossed the Cumberland Mountains. He was mostly interested in the plants and the geology, but other things drew his attention as well. He saw a South that was recovering from war. The people he encountered faced a world of poverty.

The Civil War had left the farms and people of the region poor. Farms and crops had been destroyed, and the people had little to eat or wear. Many of them wandered about without work. Some were former Confederate soldiers who had nothing to return to after the war. Others were freed slaves who now had no homes and no means of earning a living. They were all suspicious of strangers, especially strangers who weren't Southerners.

John gathered some plants and sent them home to his brother David for safekeeping. He had left most of his money with David and had arranged for his brother to send him small amounts from time to time. There were no jobs here, and John couldn't hope to find work as easily as he had during his wanderings in Canada. Most of the people were so poor that they couldn't even change large coins. If John wanted a loaf of bread, he had to have small change in order to buy it.

Some of the people John met were pleasant, but others were scary. His knowledge of the Bible came in handy at times. Once a man challenged him, saying that it wasn't right for a grown man to spend his time just studying plants. Quoting from the Bible, John said, "Consider the lilies..." The man was silenced.

The biggest problem John now faced was his declining health. By the time he reached Savannah, Georgia, he had a fever that wouldn't go away. To make matters worse, he had little money left and the money David was supposed to send hadn't arrived. There was no work for outsiders in this impoverished land.

He found a cheap hotel to stay in, but by the next day the money from David still hadn't arrived. By now John had only $1.25 in his pocket. He wandered about looking for a place to stay where no one would bother him. At the edge of town, he found Buenaventura Cemetery. Many people were superstitious about cemeteries, so no one would bother him here.

He went back into town and bought some crackers. These and some dirty ditch water were all he had for about five days. When the money from David finally arrived, John felt how good it was to walk down the street with money in his pocket again. He celebrated by buying a whole tray of gingerbread from a street vendor and gobbled the gingerbread down. He was still hungry, so he went into a restaurant for a meal before he took a boat for the west coast of Florida, on the Gulf of Mexico.

He really wanted to go to Cuba and then South America. When he discovered that the boat for Cuba wouldn't be leaving for another two weeks, he took a job in a sawmill with a Mr. Hodgson. At the mill one day, John came down with another fever and almost died. Mr. and Mrs. Hodgson took him into their home and nursed him back to health. Slowly but surely, he grew well again.

He recovered in time to catch the boat to Cuba. On the boat, everybody thought John was crazy because he stayed on deck during a storm so he could study it. He spent a month in Cuba, but his illness returned. John decided to give up the idea of going to South America for the time being.

After deliberating about what to do next, he took a boat that was heading for California. This was many years before the Panama Canal was built, so the boat went to the Isthmus of Panama. Here the passengers crossed the land by railroad and everybody boarded another boat to finish the journey.

John arrived in San Francisco, California, on March 28, 1868, took one look at the city and asked a stranger to show him the way out.

"But where do you want to go?" asked the stranger.

"Anywhere that is wild," answered John. The man thought he was crazy.

John took a ferry to Oakland and then traveled eastward and began climbing the mountains toward Yosemite. John Muir didn't know it yet, but he was about to meet the great love of his life.

5

The Mystery of the Glaciers

From the moment Muir made his way out of San Francisco into the wilderness and mountains, he felt healthy.
Gone were the fever and illness of the journey he called to as
his walk to the Gulf of Mexico.

California is blessed with two beautiful mountain
ranges. The Coast Range is on the western, or Pacific, side of
the state. The Sierra Nevada towers in the east. Between
these ranges lies the Central Valley, a region that is watered
by many rivers. The rivers of the mountains and valleys flow
into the Pacific Ocean through the Golden Gate—a narrow
body of water that divides San Francisco on the south from
Marin County on the north.

John Muir took a ferry from San Francisco east across
San Francisco Bay to Oakland. Guiding himself with his
compass, he began hiking up into the Santa Clara Mountains, then to the Central Valley. He followed the Merced
River into the Sierra Nevada and Yosemite Valley. Letters he

John Muir seated at the foot of Lower Yosemite Fall.

wrote at that time about Yosemite Valley suggest that its amazing sights may have been more than he could take in all at once.

Yosemite Valley includes some of the world's most awe-inspiring natural wonders. El Capitan, a block of stone more than 600 times Muir's height, faces Bridalveil Fall. Bridalveil tumbles 620 feet from high rocks into the valley. Farther up the Merced River is Yosemite Falls, rushing down in two sections to Yosemite Valley. North of the river is North Dome, a dome-shaped peak about as high as El Capitan. It towers above the landscape. South of North Dome and east of Tenaga Creek stands a strange peak even taller than North Dome. It is Half Dome. As the name suggests, Half Dome looks like a dome that a giant has sliced down the middle from top to bottom. Only one half of the rock dome remains.

Yosemite's trees are also amazing. Groves of "Big Trees"—sequoias—some of which have been standing for more than two thousand years, rise over two hundred feet into the sky, dominating the landscape.

John Muir spent ten days in Yosemite Valley before making his way to the farmland of the Central Valley. During this time he took several jobs—first helping to bring in the harvest on a farm, then shearing sheep, and later taming wild horses.

In the autumn he found a new job and a new friend. Pat Delaney was a former priest and miner. Now he owned a ranch. Muir worked on Delaney's ranch for a while, then he got a job herding sheep for five months for a man called Smoky Jack. It was lonely work, but it gave Muir time to observe the plants, rocks, and wildlife and to record his observations in his journal. In April he made notes about springtime in the mountains. The entire world seemed to turn green, and flowers of many colors bloomed. But by May, Muir noticed that the land had already become brown and dry.

When Muir's contract with Smoky Jack ended, Delaney, who wanted to encourage Muir's studies, offered him a chance to earn money while making scientific observations. Delaney had a large flock of sheep. Someone was needed to supervise his sheepherder, Billy, when he took the sheep into the Sierra Nevada during the hot weather. If Muir agreed to watch Billy and the sheep, Delaney would pay him and also allow him as much time as he needed to study plants and rocks.

This was an attractive offer. John needed the money, but not for himself. He had received a letter from home telling him that his sister Mary was very unhappy. Mary wanted to be an artist, and she was spending more and more time drawing. In a fit of anger one day, Daniel Muir had grabbed Mary's drawings, crumpled them, thrown them into a puddle outside the house, and trampled them. In tears, poor Mary ran off to stay with a married sister.

When Muir learned about this incident, he wrote his brother David telling him to give Mary some of the money David was still keeping for him. He then wrote to Mary telling her to use the money to go to the university and study art, botany, and music. He knew he could find a way to earn more.

Climbing the mountains with Billy, two dogs, and about two thousand sheep, Muir began to notice that the huge flock of sheep ate everything and left the ground bare. The beautiful wildflowers that he loved disappeared as soon as the sheep moved through an area. Muir began to call the sheep "hoofed locusts" because they ruined the plants in much the same way the insects descended upon the land and ate everything in their path.

Muir soon found himself thinking about what had formed the beautiful land he saw all around him. It was a mystery that he wanted to solve. He wondered what natural forces had shaped the mountains, the rivers, and the valleys. "And with what tool were they quarried and carried?" he asked. He needed clues to help him figure these things out.

One day he stood on a granite rock whose surface was so polished that it reflected the sun as if it were a mirror. Scattered about this granite surface were huge boulders. He wondered how the boulders had landed on this surface. Then he began to think about the geology he had studied at the university with Professor Carr. He had seen how glaciers had carved out the land in Wisconsin. He was pretty sure that something similar had happened here as well. These boulders, he guessed, had been carried along by a glacier and had been left standing when the glacier melted. Muir was so certain about this guess that he wrote in his journal, "A fine discovery, this!" But to confirm his hunches, Muir would have to learn more about the rocks and the land by climbing and exploring the mountains.

Several days after his "fine discovery," Muir stood looking down at Yosemite Valley from the rim. What he saw so excited him that he shouted and danced wildly. A glorious waterfall raced down the cliffs to the valley below. He wanted to look directly into the falling water. He took off his shoes and socks and walked out to the edge, but he had to get a better look. Then he saw a narrow shelf of rock, just wide enough for his heels. Common sense told him not to climb out farther, but some other instinct urged him to go on. Obeying this "other" instinct, he inched along twenty or thirty feet and gazed "down into the heart of the snowy, chanting throng of comet-like streamers" of the rushing white water.

Muir was fascinated. He didn't know how long he stood gazing at the falls, and later he couldn't remember how he managed to climb back to the top of the rock. That "other instinct" seemed to take control of his body. He began to call this instinct his "other self." In the years ahead, it would help him survive many difficult climbs in the mountains.

Although Muir's scientific studies fascinated him, he also loved the beauty of the mountains. He felt, however, that Sierra Nevada was the wrong name for this range, or group of mountains. *Sierra Nevada* means "snowy range," but there was very little snow there throughout the year. Muir thought Range of Light would have been a better name because the range shimmered with light of many different colors all year.

On August 2, 1868, Muir was sketching on North Dome when he experienced another strange feeling that was impossible to ignore. This time he had a strong premonition that Professor Butler, from Wisconsin, was in Yosemite Valley. He ran down to the valley looking for Butler but realized that he had to change his clothes. They were dirty and ragged because he had been climbing in them for several days. He went back to his camp and changed. The next morning he went out in search of the professor.

Down in the valley Muir discovered that Professor Butler was indeed registered at a nearby hotel but had gone out to look at one of the waterfalls. Muir ran four miles to find his old friend. He soon ran into one of Butler's assistants, who was suspicious of the wild-looking John Muir.

Butler had written to Muir that he would be going to California, but he hadn't told anyone that he planned to visit

Yosemite. The professor was amazed to discover his former pupil. At first he didn't recognize Muir but he was delighted to meet him in that out-of-the-way place.

The professor and his friends were even more amazed when Muir told them about the premonition that had led him to look for Butler. The two men rode on horseback back to the hotel. They talked about the land and about the strange premonition that told Muir he would find Professor Butler in Yosemite Valley that day.

Muir believed that although the premonition seemed supernatural, someday people would discover a natural explanation for such extrasensory experiences. Meanwhile, he was looking for clues to unravel a different kind of mystery. Had there been glaciers in Yosemite? Were they responsible for shaping the land? He was already certain that the answer to both questions was yes. When he and Billy took the sheep from the rim of Yosemite Valley up into the hills near Tuolumne (too OL uh mee) Meadows, northeast of the valley, he discovered more clues that confirmed his theories. He found a moraine (muh RAIN).

To understand what a moraine is, you have to know a little about the way a glacier behaves. A glacier is a river of thick ice that moves over the land very slowly. As it moves, it picks up rocks, soil, and other materials; then it deposits them along the way. The material that is deposited makes up the moraine. Most of the moraine is deposited at the sides of the glacier, but some of it is left when the glacier melts or when it meets another glacier. A geologist has no trouble recognizing a moraine because it stands out as a ridge above the other parts of the land.

Muir began tracing the path of the moraine from the place where the glacier had stopped and melted. He followed a path up into the mountains and discovered where the glacier began. There was no longer any glacier, only a moraine. This was strong evidence that a glacier had once been there.

After they brought the sheep back to the Delaney ranch that day, Muir and Delaney talked about the moraine and what it meant. Muir had fallen in love with Yosemite Valley, and he wanted to spend as much time as possible exploring the mystery of the glaciers.

Late in 1869, Muir began working at the Hutchings Hotel in Yosemite for a man named John Hutchings. Hutchings had been informing people about the valley since 1855 and had been leading tourists in to see it for many years. In 1864, he claimed land in Yosemite and built a hotel there, but he had recently run into problems.

One of Hutchings's problems was that more people were coming into the valley than ever before, and his hotel had become too small and too primitive. There were no real walls between the rooms, just curtains. Hutchings hired Muir to build a sawmill to provide wood that could be used to make rooms and new cabins. Muir agreed on one condition—that none of the trees would be cut down for the wood. He needn't have worried about that, though. There were many large trees that had fallen over during storms. The wood from these fallen trees would provide all the lumber the hotel needed.

Hutchings's other problem was more complicated. He had claimed the land at Yosemite in what he thought was a perfectly legal manner. However, the courts decided that he had not lived on the claimed land continuously for a year. In 1864, the United States gave Yosemite Valley to the state of California as a park. Nobody was sure what this meant or how it would affect Hutchings's claim. Did it mean that his land and other land that had been claimed before the park was created were now part of the park? Nobody knew for certain. Hutchings spent a lot of time in Washington, D.C., trying to prove that the land belonged to him. If it didn't belong to him, he wanted to be paid for his loss.

In the meantime, Muir built the sawmill and gathered the lumber that would be needed for the hotel. He also spent time outdoors studying his beloved rocks and plants. On New Year's Day 1870, he celebrated by climbing El Capitan. (Muir did not climb the clifflike face of El Capitan, which was not climbed on that side until 1958.) Muir used no ropes or other special equipment. He made his way down that night with some difficulty.

In April tourists began coming to Yosemite Valley, but Hutchings was still in Washington, D.C. Muir had no desire to be a guide. But he found himself showing the tourists the valley because there was no one else there who could do it. It soon became obvious to him that some of these visitors simply looked around and said "pretty" and "charming" but didn't really seem to appreciate what they saw. Muir hated guiding these people.

Other visitors were more interested in the valley. As Muir showed them the many sights, he explained how glaciers had sculptured the land. He showed them the scratches the glaciers had made, the shiny rocks they had polished, and the moraines they had deposited. These visitors listened, returned home, and began to discuss what they had seen and learned.

Some visitors pointed out that a great geologist, Josiah D. Whitney, had written that there had never been a glacier in Yosemite. Whitney was a professor at Harvard University and the chief geologist for the state of California. He had also written the guidebook for Yosemite Valley.

Muir had read some of Whitney's writings and admired

the great geologist, but he wasn't aware of Whitney's explanation of how the valley was formed. According to Whitney, Yosemite Valley was formed when an earthquake or some other natural catastrophe made the bottom of the valley sink. Whitney had written that there had never been a glacier in Yosemite or anywhere else in the Sierra Nevada.

In spite of his great admiration for Whitney, Muir was sure the geologist was wrong about the glaciers. Muir also believed that he could prove it. He thought the rocks told their own story and that people just had to understand how to read the "mountain truths." He continued to study the clues and made maps of the paths he believed the ancient glaciers had taken. Muir thought that Whitney would be more interested in scientific truth than in proving that he was right.

When Hutchings returned in May, he was furious with Muir. The tourists liked Muir, but Hutchings wanted to be the one to show them around. Hutchings was also jealous because his wife and children liked listening to Muir's nature explanations. His wife had not accompanied him to Washington. Hutchings was even more upset when he learned that Muir had disagreed with Whitney. Whitney was a great geologist. Who was Muir?

Muir wasn't unhappy about letting Hutchings guide the tourists because he had never wanted to do it in the first place. But certain visitors came looking for him because friends had sent them. The friends who sent most of the visitors were Professor and Mrs. Carr. Years ago, Professor Carr had welcomed Muir into his home and invited him to use his library. Jeanne Carr had recognized Muir's unusual ability and insight when she saw the device he made to measure a plant's growth. She and Muir had been exchanging ideas in their letters to each other for several years. The

Jeanne Carr. Since the early 1860s, she had played an important part in urging John Muir to continue his studies and writing.

two friends shared a great love of plants and the world of nature. More important, Jeanne Carr believed in John Muir.

Professor Carr now taught at the University of California. The Carr family lived in San Francisco, and many scientists, writers, and professors visited the Carrs before going on to Yosemite, and they were all told to look for John Muir and ask him to show them around. One such visitor was Joseph Le Conte, a professor at the University of California. He arrived at Yosemite with nine students. As they rode through Yosemite together, Muir convinced the professor that glaciers had carved out the valley. The two men became friends, and Le Conte returned to the city full of Muir's ideas about the effects of glaciers on Yosemite.

When Whitney, the great geologist, heard people discussing Muir's ideas, he exclaimed, "What does that sheepherder know about it?"

Because of his disagreement with Hutchings, Muir had returned to work for his friend Delaney for a while. But Hutchings soon asked him to return. The cabin Muir had built for himself had become a home for Hutchings's sister, so Muir had to build a new one. This time he built his home under the gable of the sawmill, facing Yosemite Falls. He called the place "a hang-bird's hang-nest." People had to climb a ladder to get in. That discouraged many would-be visitors.

Muir had gradually become convinced that there were still glaciers in Yosemite, and he went in search of them. "I will follow my instincts," he said, "be myself for good or ill."

Meanwhile, in San Francisco a very special visitor came to see Jeanne Carr. Ralph Waldo Emerson, the great poet and writer and a friend of the Carrs, was on his way to Yosemite. Although Emerson didn't get to see Mrs. Carr, she wrote him a note telling him to look up John Muir at

Yosemite. Then she wrote to Muir telling him that Emerson was on his way and asking him to look out for him.

Muir had always admired Emerson. The writer wrote about nature and people. Emerson encouraged people to rely on themselves and their beliefs, and Muir agreed with him. Muir was looking forward to the visit. But when Emerson arrived, he came with a large group of followers from Massachusetts. At the hotel, so many people crowded around the great man that Muir was shy about approaching him. But when he learned that Emerson would be leaving within a few days, he wrote a note and gave it to one of the writer's friends. In the note Muir wrote: "Do not drift away with the mob while the spirits of these rocks and waters hail you....I invite you to join me in a month's worship with Nature in the high temples of the great Sierra Crown beyond our holy Yosemite."

The next morning, Ralph Waldo Emerson rode up to the sawmill where Muir was hard at work. Muir helped the writer up the ladder to his "hang-nest" and showed Emerson his rocks and plants. Muir spoke of the glaciers and the natural forces in the valley. Then he asked Emerson to go camping with him. But Emerson was now in his sixties, and his companions feared that he might not be strong enough for the trip.

The two men spoke often. When Emerson left, Muir rode with him to the Mariposa Grove, an area of Big Trees, and they said good-bye. Afterward Muir felt very lonely. Emerson was someone who shared many of his own ideas. Later they wrote to each other, and Muir often sent plant samples to the great writer.

At his home, Emerson kept a short list of "My Men." They were the men whom Emerson most admired. The last name he placed on the list was John Muir. Like Jeanne Carr and Joseph Le Conte, Ralph Waldo Emerson urged John Muir to put his ideas into writing. So far, the only writing Muir had done was in his journals and in the many letters he wrote to friends and family. His friends felt that it was time he began writing articles so that more people could learn about his discoveries and experiences. But Muir didn't want to spend his time writing.

He also didn't want to leave Yosemite and go into the city, but Jeanne Carr had begun to worry about him. She thought he was becoming a wild mountain man. He needed to stay in the city for a while to get some polish, she said. He also needed to discuss his ideas with other people who understood his work. With this in mind, she sent John Runkle to Yosemite. Runkle was the president of the Massachusetts Institute of Technology. He listened to Muir and urged him to go to Boston to teach. At the very least, Runkle insisted, Muir should write up his ideas about glaciers.

Muir had begun to express his ideas in the letters he wrote to Runkle and others. Finally, he used the ideas he had written in these letters to write an article called "The Death of a Glacier." Muir sent the article to the *New York Tribune*, and to his amazement, the newspaper editors accepted the article and paid him for it. They wanted him to write more articles. For the first time, John Muir realized that he might earn money by writing.

On October 6, 1871, Muir was climbing between the Red and Black mountains (now called Red Peak and Merced Peak). He saw clues that a glacier had been there. Then he saw something completely different. "Glacial mud!" he wrote. "A living glacier!" Glaciers carried mud as well as rocks and soil when they traveled. Glacial mud is the ground-up rock at the front edge of a glacier, and Muir traced it to its beginning. He had found a real, living glacier right in

This is one of the many drawings John Muir made in his journals.

Yosemite, but he still had more work to do to prove his findings.

Winter came. Once Muir tried to climb up a canyon after a snowfall to study some avalanches. He thought it would take him three or four hours to get to the top, but he had been climbing most of the day and he still hadn't reached the top. Suddenly an avalanche started. He wrote: "I was swished down to the foot of the canyon as if by enchantment. The wallowing ascent [climb up] had taken nearly all day, the descent [fall down] only about a minute. When the avalanche started I threw myself on my back and spread my arms to try to keep from sinking." He ended by saying, "This was a fine experience."

In December there was a wild storm, and Muir went out in it to observe and enjoy it. On March 26, 1872, a powerful earthquake came to the valley. While everyone else was trying to get away, Muir stood outside to enjoy the earthquake. Everyone thought he was crazy. He had climbed onto some of the boulders while they were still moving down the slopes.

One summer Professor Catherine Merrill sent her nephew Merrill Moores, who was now sixteen, to visit Muir. Together man and boy went to measure the flow of the glacier Muir had found. Muir used the method he had learned by reading the works of Louis Agassiz. He placed some sticks upright in the ice and others upright in the land. Later he went back to measure how far the glacier had moved.

As a result of Muir's articles, famous scientists began to visit him in Yosemite. John Tyndall, a British expert on glaciers was one of these scientists. He was very impressed with Muir's work. When Tyndall left, he sent Muir scientific instruments that would allow him to continue his work.

Another visitor was Asa Gray, a botanist from Harvard University. Muir and Gray had been writing to each other and exchanging plant samples for some time. Gray wanted Muir to return with him to Harvard to teach, but Muir wasn't interested. Gray later named a newly discovered plant, *Ivesia Murii*, for his friend John Muir.

The great Louis Agassiz himself reached San Francisco in August 1872. Muir wrote to Agassiz urging him to visit Yosemite and see what he had discovered, but Agassiz was sick and wasn't up to making the journey. His wife wrote to John explaining the situation. In her letter she wrote that

Agassiz had said of Muir's work on glaciers, "Here is the first man who has any adequate conception [idea] of glacial action." In addition, Agassiz had been Joseph Le Conte's teacher. When Le Conte told his former professor that Muir knew more about the Sierra's glaciers than anybody else, Agassiz replied, "He knows *all* about it!"

When Muir went back to examine his glacier, he discovered that the sticks now formed a curve. The sticks in the center had moved ahead of those on the sides. He realized that this meant that the speed at which the center of a glacier moved was greater than that of the sides.

Despite the fact that Muir had discovered a living glacier at Yosemite and had measured its movement, Josiah Whitney still insisted that there were no glaciers in Yosemite or anywhere else in the Sierra Nevada. Until the end, he never accepted Muir's work with glaciers. Yet today, scientists do not accept Whitney's theory of how Yosemite Valley was formed.

It took many years for most scientists to recognize that glaciers had helped form Yosemite. John Muir's work with glaciers is now widely accepted. For the most part, his theories were right. Glaciers did a great deal of the work in shaping the land, but they weren't the only natural force at work. Scientists today believe that both rivers and glaciers helped carve the wonders of Yosemite.

6

"How Shall We Preserve Our Forests?"

Three artists—all Scotsmen—came to visit Muir at Yosemite. One of them, William Keith, became his lifelong friend. The artists wanted Muir to show them views of Yosemite that would be good for painting. Muir also gave them information about the plants and rocks in the valley, that might enhance their paintings.

Muir left his friends to their drawing one day and went off to climb the black crags of Mount Ritter. As far as he knew, no one had managed to climb to the very top of this mountain. He climbed part of the way and decided to camp for the night near a lake and waterfall.

In the morning he began to climb in earnest. He crossed a glacier and carefully scaled the rocks, using the cracks and joints in the surface for handholds and footholds. He then zigzagged across the ice-covered peak, but as he climbed he found fewer and fewer places for his hands and feet. Finally he reached a spot where there were no more handholds or footholds. He was unable to move.

Muir broke out into a cold sweat when he realized what a dangerous position he was in. Thoughts of falling to the glacier below were uppermost in his mind when his "other self" took over.

I became possessed of a new sense. My quivering nerves, taken over by my other self, instinct, or guardian angel—call it what you will—became inflexible. My eyes became preternaturally [unnaturally] clear, and every rift, flaw, niche, and tablet in the cliff ahead, were seen as through a microscope. At any rate the danger was safely passed, I scarce know how, and shortly after noon I leaped with wild freedom, into the sunlight upon the highest crag of the summit. Had I been borne [carried] aloft upon wings, my deliverance could not have been more complete.

As the sun began to set, Muir descended Mount Ritter and returned to the campsite he had made the night before. He fell asleep to the sound of the waterfall. The next day he joined his artist friends. They had been worried about his safety, but they needn't have been. Without using any special equipment, except items he himself had invented, John Muir climbed mountains that many skilled mountaineers today find difficult even with the finest modern equipment. But Muir's ability to climb was more than just skill. He had learned to trust nature. He had become a part of the wilderness and was perfectly in tune with its laws.

Muir also had his own way of dressing when he went out for a climb. He usually wore a wool shirt, a vest, and a jacket, but no overcoat. He kept scientific instruments in his vest pockets. For food, he usually took bread or crackers and oatmeal. He wore shoes with thick soles, never boots. He tried to begin his climb early—before sunup—so that he could return the same day. That way, he didn't have to worry about spending a cold night at the mountaintop. If he had to start a fire, however, he always had whatever he needed.

Muir's artist friends talked him into returning to the San Francisco area with them when they left Yosemite. For two "municipal weeks," he traveled back and forth across the bay between the cities of San Francisco and Oakland, visiting the Carrs, the McChesneys, the Le Contes, the Keiths, and other friends. But city life was more than he could tolerate at the time. He was eager to return to the wilderness.

When Muir returned to the mountains after his trip to the city, he had difficulty climbing. On one of these climbs he hit his head and fell down a steep cliff. Fortunately, his fall was cushioned by some frail bushes. Was this another "guardian angel" protecting him? he wondered. Annoyed with himself for falling, Muir forced himself to climb the same mountain again. This time his old skill returned as he climbed.

Many changes were taking place in John Muir's life at this time. He was becoming a serious writer, and before long, he had promised to write about fifteen articles. In the meantime, though, he worried about his family in Wisconsin. His father had sold the land and planned to move to England to work with a group that said it worked with the poor and sick.

John wrote to his brother David and his brother-in-law David Galloway asking them to convince his father to change his plans. The two Davids succeeded in talking Daniel Muir into going to Canada instead of England. In Canada, Daniel

Muir happily continued his preaching and worked with sick people. His wife remained in Portage, Wisconsin, to be near some of her children.

Muir also found himself worrying about the *ecology*—the relationship between living things and their surroundings and to each other—of Yosemite. More and more sheep were coming into the mountains to graze, and they were destroying the plants. Muir realized that if this continued, the land could be destroyed for good.

The Big Trees were also in trouble. Tourists who poured into the "Giant Forest" area, about thirty-five miles south of Yosemite Valley, had no respect for the giant trees. Many carved their names on the great trunks. One tree, called the General Grant, had been gouged with these carvings.

Muir soon realized that human beings could be dangerous to the wilderness. He wondered how nature could be saved from people's greed and carelessness. He didn't yet know what he could do to solve this problem.

One freezing night Muir tried to climb Mount Whitney (named for Josiah D. Whitney) in a severe gale. By the time he reached the top of a nearby mountain (now called Mount Muir), the temperature was 22°F below zero. Muir had no coat or blanket, but by now he knew how to survive in the coldest wilderness. He knew he had to stay awake in order to stay alive, so he spent the night dancing Scottish dances, singing songs, and swinging his arms and clapping his hands to keep them from becoming numb.

In the morning, he again tried to climb to the top, but his "other self" told him to go back. Although he was disappointed, he obeyed his instincts and made his way back down the mountain. All his life, Muir believed that natural forces guided him. Writing about these forces, he once said that "we are governed more than we know, and most when we are wildest."

Muir later did succeed in climbing Mount Whitney. Two men had climbed the mountain before him and had left their names at the top. Muir left nothing to mark his presence on Mount Whitney, but he did mention it in his journal. He would have liked to spend the winter in the mountains, but he had a great deal of writing to do. Reluctantly, he returned to the city for the winter.

Jeanne Carr still worried about Muir. She kept urging him to be more social. She said, "You must be social, John, you must make friends...."

Yet John Muir knew that he had made many friends. While writing his articles, he stayed in Oakland with his friends the McChesneys for a while. He worked hard at his writing, which he found very difficult. Each time he began to write about one thing, it seemed there were hundreds of others that would be just as interesting.

Some of Muir's articles were published in *Overland Monthly*, a California magazine that had been started by the writer Bret Harte. These articles were about Muir's exploration of the mountains. Jeanne Carr advised him to write in a way that would make his studies interesting to scientists as well as to ordinary readers. At the same time, because the scientists had to take Muir seriously, his writing had to cut back on poetic enthusiasm.

Over the years, Muir developed a unique style of writing. Unlike most scientists, who try to write impersonally, his work is usually very personal and enthusiastic. He was always careful to be accurate about scientific data, but he tried to write the way Ralph Waldo Emerson and Henry David Thoreau wrote.

As the years went by many new people entered Muir's

life. He visited Joseph Le Conte and Joseph's brother John, who was also a professor, and discussed glaciers with them. Through the Carrs, he met John and Mary Swett. Swett, who had been the superintendent of California's schools, was responsible for setting up the state's school system. He was now a school principal and became one of Muir's closest friends.

One day while Muir was visiting the Carrs, Dr. John Strentzel and his family stopped by. Strentzel had left his native Poland for political reasons and now lived in the United States. He had a large fruit ranch northeast of San Francisco. The scientific methods he used to grow his fruits had given them a reputation for being very high in quality.

Mrs. Strentzel had been following Muir's articles in the *Overland Monthly* and was glad to meet him at last. Long before her visit to the Carrs, she had written in her diary: "How I should love to become acquainted with a person who writes as he does. What is wealth compared to a mind like his! And yet I shall probably never see him."

The Strentzels had a daughter, Louisa "Louie" Wanda, whom Jeanne Carr had tried to introduce to Muir. But until now, Muir had managed to avoid every opportunity to meet the young woman.

Louie was an outstanding pianist, but her father had taught her a lot about botany. She was responsible for a great deal of the business of the fruit ranch. Although many men had proposed to Louie Wanda, she had shown no interest in any of them. Jeanne Carr hoped that Louie would be interested enough in John Muir to "take him out of the wilderness into the society of his peers." The Strentzels asked John to visit their ranch. Although he said he might come, it was several years before he kept his promise.

In September, with his articles finished, Muir returned to Yosemite. He had by then discovered nearly all the glaciers in the Sierra Nevada range. He found that he no longer had any reason to continue working with the glaciers there and he decided to move on. He went on to Mount Shasta, a mountain that had once been a volcano. He was outraged to discover that the forests along the way had been "hacked and smashed." Once again, he began to worry about the damage people were doing to the wilderness.

Next he went through Donner Pass, the site where a group of pioneers moving to California in 1846–47 had been trapped in a snowstorm. They had run out of food, and many of them had died.

As Muir looked around the area, he saw many ways in which the Donner party could have survived if only they had understood the wilderness. He felt that if they hadn't been so removed from nature, they could have spent a delightful winter there in a beautiful spot. Muir's skills for surviving in the wilderness were so natural to him that he may not have realized just how rare they were.

At Mount Shasta, Muir traced the paths made by lava flowing from the volcano as well as those made by glaciers. When he began to make his way down from the mountain, he ran into three days of a "glorious storm." On the fourth day, he met a worried guide who had been looking for him. Muir was annoyed that the guide thought he might be in trouble.

Emily Pelton, Muir's old friend from Prairie du Chien, was now living in California. The two of them had been writing to each other for many years. John stopped by to visit her. While he was there, there was a big storm. He thought it would be a good idea to climb a tree to get a wider view of the storm and listen to the sounds at the top of the tree. He chose a Douglas spruce, about 100 feet high, as his lookout point.

> In its widest sweeps my tree-top described an arc of from twenty to thirty degrees, but I felt sure of its elastic temper, having seen others of the same species...bent almost to the ground indeed in heavy snows—without breaking a fiber. I was therefore safe, and free to take the wind into my pulses and enjoy the excited forest from my superb outlook.

Muir enjoyed the sounds, the "profound bass of the naked branches," "the quick, tense vibrations of the pine-needles," and the "keen metallic click of leaf on leaf." But Emily was very upset at his behavior.

After leaving Emily Pelton, John Muir returned to Oakland to stay with John Swett. Swett and William Keith, Muir's artist friend who lived nearby, began to persuade Muir to write an article on glaciers for a magazine in the East. They explained that easterners hardly ever read western magazines or newspapers but that many educated people throughout the country read magazines that were published in eastern cities.

As a result, Muir rewrote an article about glaciers for *Harper's* magazine. More and more people in the United States were beginning to hear of John Muir's ideas through his writing.

Even as he wrote about the wilderness, however, Muir worried about how long the wilderness would last. Swett belonged to a group of people who were concerned that powerful individuals were gaining control of large forest and water areas. When Muir heard his friends discussing their

John Muir in Yosemite Valley.

concerns, he realized that they were all concerned about the same issues in different ways. Muir realized that if the water in the mountains was controlled by a few people, the valleys might not get any. Similarly if the forests were chopped down, there would be no wild plants and animals.

In September 1875, Muir returned to Yosemite and his worries increased. "Yosemite is doomed to perish," he wrote. He saw that sawmill workers near the valley had chopped down many of the giant sequoia trees. To make matters worse, the sawmill operators had used less than half the wood and had wasted the rest. As he rode his mule Brownie up the mountains, Muir saw how sheep had destroyed the grass. He had to rush down the mountain to buy a bag of barley for Brownie because there was no grass for the animal to eat.

Muir soon returned to San Francisco, where he wrote several articles for the *San Francisco Bulletin*. He was beginning to realize that his writing could draw attention to the wilderness that he loved so dearly. If people loved it, they would want to help save it. But it wasn't enough to save Yosemite; Muir wanted to save all the wild places of the nation and the world.

In January 1876, Muir wrote his first article asking the government to take charge of the forests. It appeared in the Sacramento *Record-Union* under the title "God's First Temples—How Shall We Preserve Our Forests?" In the article, Muir described himself as a "practical man." He pointed out that European countries had destroyed most of their forests and the United States was following in their footsteps.

John Muir had become a conservationist—someone who wants to save our natural resources so that future generations, too, can enjoy them. Conservation was the work for which Muir would be best known.

CHAPTER

7

Louie and the Ice Chief

By now, John Muir was approaching his fortieth birthday. He thoroughly enjoyed his studies of glaciers, rocks, and plants. When he wasn't occupied with his studies, he shared the companionship of good friends. His writing had attracted a growing audience of admiring readers. Yet he often felt lonely.

Muir loved children and always managed to gain their affection. In fact, when he stayed at the home of John and Mary Swett, their baby daughter played in his room while he wrote. Often he found himself wondering what it would be like to have a family of his own. In a letter to his sister Sarah he wrote that he had never intended to live as a bachelor.

Many women liked and admired John Muir, and he was probably aware of their interest. But how could he live in the mountains and still be a husband and father? Like Emily Pelton, most women wouldn't understand why he wanted to go out into a storm or an earthquake just to study it and

83

experience it. Besides, he felt healthy in the mountains and couldn't abide city living for long periods of time. It seemed that he would remain a bachelor for the rest of his life.

These thoughts were on his mind when Muir went to Utah to study more plants and to look for evidence of old glaciers. After stopping at Lake Tahoe and at Yosemite, he returned to San Francisco with a new project in mind. He wanted to study the coast redwoods the way he had studied the giant sequoias. (The coast redwoods grow in the fog belt along the coast of California and southern Oregon.) But a surprise visit from Asa Gray, the Harvard botanist, and Gray's wife forced him to change his plans. Sir Joseph Hooker, a famous English botanist, had also come to meet Muir. The botanists wanted Muir to take them through Yosemite. Before the group set off, General John Bidwell—a prominent Californian and former U.S. congressman—and his wife and sister-in-law joined them.

Soon after their trip through Yosemite, the Grays departed with Sir Joseph, and Muir returned with the Bidwells to their ranch. From there he soon set out on another adventure, floating down the Merced River in a small skiff. Toward the end of his trip, Muir found himself near the town of Martinez, about twenty miles northeast of Oakland. Tired and hungry, Muir remembered that Martinez was the home of the Strentzel family. He decided that it was time he accepted their invitation to visit.

The "Strentzel Trinity," as Muir called the family, were gracious hosts. After providing him with a hearty meal, they sat together and talked. Then they gave him a bedroom with the softest sheets he had ever slept on.

When Muir left the Strentzels, he hiked most of the way back to San Francisco, where he stayed with the Swetts. He was full of wonderful stories to tell the Swett children. He told them about the Douglas squirrel (one of his favorite animals) and the water ouzel (OO-zul), his favorite bird. Each time Muir told one of these stories, Mrs. Swett said, "Now John, go upstairs and write that down just as you have told it to us."

He sent many of these stories to *Scribner's*, a magazine whose readers enjoyed his work. *Scribner's* wanted Muir to write more of these stories. These tales and an article in *Harper's* magazine about the redwoods made John Muir a nationally known writer.

During this time, Muir made many visits to the Strentzels. Although he told his San Francisco friends that he was spending time with Dr. and Mrs. Strentzel, he was also spending many hours talking and walking about the hills with their daughter, Louie Wanda. When Muir wasn't visiting the Strentzels at their fruit ranch, he often kept in touch by writing to them.

Muir's next project was a trip to Nevada where he participated in a geodetic survey—scientific work to measure the land. There, he saw many ghost towns, places that had once been booming mining towns but were now deserted because the mines had closed. All that was left were empty buildings.

While making his way back to Martinez, Muir stopped at Yosemite. He had been asked to give two lectures to a Sunday school convention there and to lead a few tours through the valley.

Muir was not the only speaker at the convention. Joseph Cook, a famous lecturer, was also scheduled to talk. To prepare for his talk, Cook had done background research by reading Josiah D. Whitney's book about Yosemite, and in his speech he explained Whitney's theory of how the valley was formed.

Cook's speaking style was that of a grand orator. When it was Muir's turn, he didn't argue with Cook. Instead, he thanked the lecturer and said he couldn't hope to speak as well. Then he calmly talked about his years in the mountains, telling the audience what he had discovered about glaciers.

The next day, Cook joined Muir's tour of Glacier Point Trail. Muir pointed out the clues that had led to his understanding of Yosemite and how it was formed. At the end of the tour, Cook realized that Muir was right. Although he said nothing to Muir, Cook gave another lecture on Yosemite a few days later, and in it he described Muir's theory.

When Muir visited the Strentzels after his talk at Yosemite, it was obvious that something had changed between him and Louie.

Later that night Louie told her mother, "All's well, Mother. All's well, and I'm so happy." She and Muir had decided to marry, but their plans would remain secret for a while.

Before the wedding, Muir wanted to visit Alaska. He took a boat to Puget Sound on the Pacific coast of the state of Washington. From there he boarded the steamship *California*. The other three passengers on board were members of the Presbyterian Board of Missionaries who were going to Alaska to inspect missionary activities. They didn't approve of Muir and called him "that wild Muir." He didn't like them much either. Perhaps their religious views reminded him of his father's uncompromising beliefs.

The *California* stopped in southeastern Alaska at the small Native American settlement of Fort Wrangell, where Muir met a young missionary named S. Hall Young, who lived and worked there. Muir and Young took one look at each other, and each recognized a possible friend. When the missionaries, including Young, took a river steamer north to try to convert the Chilcat Indians, Muir went with them. On the way, in conversations with the engineer, Muir learned that lumber companies were seizing large areas of the forest by dishonest means.

The river steamer couldn't continue north because of ice, so the boat turned and went eastward up the Stickeen River.

When the boat docked for a short stay at Glenora, Muir and Young looked at each other, and their glances seemed to say, "Let's explore." They went off to climb Glenora Peak. At first Muir worried that the climb would be too much for Young, but the missionary assured him that he was an experienced climber. As they made their way up the slope, Muir saw that Young was a "stout walker" and realized that there was no cause for concern. Young, in turn, was amazed at Muir's climbing skill and soon began to imitate him.

Young was fascinated by the way Muir stopped to look at the flowers they saw as they climbed. Muir spoke to these flowers in an affectionate mixture of baby talk and scientific language that amazed Young. As Muir and Young hurried to catch the sunset at the top of the mountain, they reached a ledge that was about fifty feet from the top. Muir shouted to Young, "Be very careful here, this is dangerous." Young didn't hear Muir.

Young leaped and landed on a stone that crumbled under his feet. His screams echoed through the mountain. Muir found him lying face down with his arms outstretched on a ledge. Young wondered how long it would take for him to fall through the air to the glacier below. He thought about his wife, whom he feared he would never see again.

Muir made his way to a point below his friend and

quietly said, "I am below you. You are in no danger. You can't slip past me, and I will soon get you out of this."

Young's shoulders had been dislocated in an accident when he was a teenager, and now they were dislocated again. He couldn't use his arms. Muir grabbed his friend by the belt and clothing and pulled him away from the edge. Then he helped Young down to the glacier a thousand feet below, talking reassuringly and singing to calm him.

Muir tried to set Young's arms but found the dislocation too difficult to deal with at that time. He offered to build a fire and go for help, but Young didn't want to be left alone. Slowly they made their way back to the ship, stopping whenever they could to build fires and to rest.

When they finally reached the steamer, Mr. Kendall, one of the missionaries, said, "These foolish adventures are well enough for Mr. Muir, but you, Mr. Young, have a work to do; you have a family; you have a church, and you have no right to risk your life on treacherous peaks and precipices."

The boat's captain grew angry at Kendall and told him that it was no time for preaching; the man was hurt. Even Mrs. Kendall thought her husband was wrong.

"Henry Kendall," she said angrily, "shut right up and leave this room. Have you no sense?"

Young survived his brush with death and loved to tell the story of how Muir had saved his life. S. Hall Young remained one of John Muir's greatest friends and admirers. He even wrote a book called *Alaska Days with John Muir*. Young once said of his friend, "I have camped with many men, but have never found his equal as a man of the wilderness."

When the steamer returned to Fort Wrangell, the Native Americans there, who had recently become Christians, held a dance to celebrate. They adopted John Muir and gave him an Indian name.

It was already October, and Muir hadn't finished exploring the glaciers. There were several mysteries he wanted to solve about sudden floods in glacial areas. He had heard that there were glaciers to the north, and he hired one of the Native Americans, Chief Toyatte, and his thirty-six-foot canoe to take him and Young north. Chief Toyatte and his Native American crew took their passengers part of the way and then refused to continue any farther. They had heard many terrible tales about the northern glaciers and the monsters that supposedly lived in the north.

Muir, who by now had been nicknamed the Ice Chief because of his knowledge of glaciers, told the crew that he had escaped death many times because a guardian spirit watched over him. He told them about some of his adventures and about his "other self." He said, "You will have good luck when you travel with me." The Native Americans were so moved by his words that they took courage and agreed to go on.

At the glacial site, Muir crawled underneath a huge glacier to see what was taking place on the underside. He was able to see how a glacier picked up huge rocks and carried them along. The party came to one enormous glacier that was later named Muir Glacier.

The Ice Chief wanted to study one more glacier, but winter was approaching. The passengers could see the next glacier looming ahead, but Chief Toyatte said now they really had to return to town. Muir later called this glacier that he didn't explore his "Lost Glacier."

One important discovery Muir made was that the region's shoreline was changing. The map he used on this voyage had been drawn in 1794. It didn't show the bay and its glaciers as they appeared in 1879. Muir made several predictions about how the glaciers would sculpture the land and alter coastline in the future. Changes that have taken place since 1879 show that most of Muir's predictions have proved to be accurate.

When the party returned to Fort Wrangell in December, Muir found a letter from Louie waiting for him. She said that she hoped he would be home for Thanksgiving, but it was already too late for that.

Before returning to Martinez, Muir stopped to give some lectures for which he was well paid. He wanted to have some money when he returned to Louie. On April 14, 1880, John Muir and Louie Wanda Strentzel were married at the Strentzel ranch. The walls of the house were covered with flowers and branches. As a wedding gift, Dr. and Mrs. Strentzel gave the newlyweds the house they had lived in and twenty acres of orchard. They would build a larger home, the Big House, for themselves in another part of the ranch. Jeanne Carr and many other friends sent letters and telegrams congratulating the newlyweds. John wrote back to Mrs. Carr, "I am now the happiest man on earth."

Muir was determined to make a success of both his marriage and the ranch. The morning after the wedding, he was already busy working in the orchard. But Louie knew that her husband couldn't live without the wilderness, so they made an agreement. From July to October, when the ranch required little work, John could go out exploring. When autumn came, he would return to help with the grape harvest.

In July, Muir left for Alaska once again. This time he was determined to study the "Lost Glacier." Young was delighted to see Muir again. "When can you be ready?" Muir asked his friend.

Unfortunately, Chief Toyatte had been killed since Muir's last visit. He was sorry to learn of his old friend's death. As soon as they were able to find another Native American with a boat Muir and Young prepared to explore. The boat was about to depart when Young's dog Stickeen leaped on board. Muir tried to get the dog to leave, but the animal refused to go.

As they sailed along, Muir saw signs that changes were taking place rapidly. Many glaciers were becoming smaller. One was growing larger. On August 21, they reached the "Lost Glacier," and Muir had his chance to explore it. Then on August 29, the boat reached Taylor Glacier, the site of one of Muir's best-known adventures.

The story began when Muir went out early in the morning to explore Taylor Glacier. Stickeen, the dog, insisted on following him. All during the trip, the little dog had become increasingly fond of Muir, who tried hard to discourage him.

"Go back and get your breakfast," Muir shouted gruffly at the dog. But the dog "begged with his tail and his eyes."

Muir gave Stickeen a crust of bread and set off over the ice. After traveling for some time over the "flame-shaped waves of ice," Muir noticed that the dog's feet were bleeding. He wrapped Stickeen's feet with bandages. Several times Muir had to stop and take care of the dog's feet.

When a storm came up, both man and dog took shelter behind a tree. The storm let up and the pair continued, but night was approaching. Muir and Stickeen had to jump across several crevasses—huge cracks in the ice. At last they reached one that was too wide to cross. Now Muir and the dog found themselves in danger of being stranded on an island of ice with no means of escape.

Muir looked for a way out and noticed what he called a "sliver bridge" of ice hanging like a loose rope. Their only hope was for him to use his ice ax to cut steps across this very narrow bridge. He made a path four inches wide for Stickeen.

The dog inspected what the man was doing, then turned and whined as if to say, "Surely you are not going down there."

Muir insisted, "Yes, Stickeen, this is the only way."

The unhappy dog cried and whined and tried to find another way. When he couldn't, he returned to Muir, lay down, and cried even louder.

Muir used a reassuring tone of voice to encourage Stickeen to make the crossing, but the dog wouldn't stop crying. In his writing, Muir described what happened next: "I told him that I must go, that he could come if he only tried, and finally in despair he hushed his cries, slid his little feet slowly down into my footsteps" and cautiously made his way across.

When the dog reached the other side, he ran and barked for joy. By the time the pair reached the camp, Young and the others had given up on them.

Instead of leaping in his usual frisky way, Stickeen walked in weakly at Muir's heels. Even Muir was exhausted. He had something to eat and said, "Yon's a brave doggie." As Muir told his companions of the dangers he and Stickeen had faced, the dog went over and laid his head on Muir's foot.

Muir would tell this story often for many years, and he eventually wrote a book titled *Stickeen*. He believed that this experience proved that animals have individual personalities and some can exhibit great loyalty and courage.

When Muir and his companions reached the port of Sitka, in southeastern Alaska, he received a letter from Louie telling him that she had been seriously ill shortly after he left home. But she had refused to let her father send for him. She wrote, "I shall not fail you when your heart has need of me."

Sadly, Muir said good-bye to his friends and Stickeen and left for home.

He was glad to be back with Louie. He soon learned that he was about to become a father. Annie Wanda was born on March 25, 1881. Muir worked hard on the ranch, but his health began to suffer. Yet when he was invited to take part in a voyage on the *Thomas Corwin* to look for the lost steamer *Jeannette* and its crew, he refused to go. Dr. Strentzel was pleased, but Louie understood what the trip meant to her husband and she insisted that he go.

In May, the *Corwin* left with Muir aboard. He had many opportunities to study glaciers and other natural features during the voyage, but the trip failed to achieve its main purpose. Those aboard the *Corwin* never spotted the *Jeannette*. In the end, only a few of the *Jeannette*'s crew survived.

By October, Muir was home again. In addition to his work on the ranch he wrote government reports about the Arctic, helped the *Corwin*'s captain write his report, and sent plant samples from the Arctic to Asa Gray at Harvard. More important, Muir was helping to draft two bills for Congress. One of these bills was a proposal to enlarge the land area that was included in the grants for Yosemite Valley and the Mariposa Big Tree Grove. The other proposed that a national public park be set aside in the southern Sierra

Nevada. The bills didn't pass, but they were the beginning of Muir's efforts to establish national parks to preserve the land.

Several family concerns now weighed on Muir's mind. Dr. Strentzel's health was failing, and Muir took over most of the work on the fruit ranch. He selected the fruits that proved most successful and grew only those. Under his supervision, the Strentzel fruit ranch became more prosperous than it ever had been.

As a counterbalance to Muir's worries, little Wanda was a joy to her father. He loved to teach her the names of flowers, and he insisted that she use them. "For how would you like it," he asked, "if people didn't call you by your name?"

Soon, several pieces of bad news arrived. First, David Galloway, his sister Sarah's husband, had died. Then he learned that his sister Annie had tuberculosis. Finally he heard that his brother David's wife had also died. Muir wanted to go to his family, but Louie was expecting another child and he didn't want to leave her at that time. Then something happened that forced him to go. He had a premonition that he had to see his father while Daniel Muir was still alive.

Muir set out for Wisconsin and reached Portage at the end of August. His brother David, sister Annie, and sister Sarah and her daughters were now living with their mother. John asked Annie to return to California with him. He hoped the air would help her heal.

In September, John, David, and Annie reached Kansas City, where their ailing father was living with their youngest sister, Joanna. John Muir sent for the rest of the family. On October 6, 1885, Daniel Muir died with seven of his eight children at his side.

After John Muir returned to California, he no longer visited the mountains or the glaciers. Helen Muir, his second child, was born on January 23, 1886. Because her health was frail, Muir didn't want to leave her.

During this time, Muir received many requests for articles about protecting the forests. His friends wanted to involve him in his former activities. Muir tried unsuccessfully to get his brother-in-law John Reid or his brother David to manage the ranch so that he would be free to take part in some of these activities. He eventually accepted a job of preparing two volumes of nature studies called *Picturesque California*, but his writing had lost its enthusiasm.

Louie was worried about her husband. She knew that he needed to get back to the wilderness. She referred to the years Muir spent on the ranch as his "seven lost years."

CHAPTER

8

The Sierra Club and a National Park

One morning in May 1888, S. Hall Young showed up at the Muir ranch. He hadn't written to say that he was coming.

"Ah! my friend," said Muir. "You have come to take me on a canoe trip..." Muir went on to tell Young that he had grown weary of the "humdrum, work-a-day life" with grapes, which he called "these miserable little bald-heads."

Young, however, had only come for a short visit. Meanwhile, though, Louie was secretly planning to get her husband back to the mountains. In June, she persuaded him to travel with a friend to Lake Tahoe, high in the Sierra Nevada, along the California-Nevada border. In July, Muir went mountain climbing with William Keith, his artist friend. Together they climbed Mount Shasta and Mount Rainier, and Muir tackled Mount Hood alone.

Although the trip into the mountains restored Muir's spirits in many ways, it also brought to his attention new problems. Forests were being destroyed for wood, and new trees weren't replacing the old ones.

By this time, John Muir and other scientists were beginning to understand that the valleys, where many people lived, depended on the mountain forests for water. Muir's studies showed him that tree roots held water in the ground. When these trees were lost, the soil could no longer hold the water and the resulting floods deluged the valleys below. If the mountains were stripped of their trees, the valleys would certainly lose their dependable water supply.

The letters Muir wrote to his wife while he was away showed her just how desperately he needed to be back in the mountains. In one letter, he told of arriving, sick from bad food, at Mount Rainier. "Did not mean to climb it," wrote John, "but got excited, and soon was on top."

Louie now knew what she had to do. While John was away, she sold part of their farmland and leased other parts. She did this so that he would have time to write the books he had planned about Alaska and Yosemite. "A ranch that needs and takes the sacrifice of a noble life, or work, ought to be flung away beyond all reach and power for harm," she wrote to her husband. "There is nothing that has a right to be considered beside this except the welfare of our children."

When he returned home, Muir started writing again. Often he took a room in a small hotel in San Francisco so that he could work without being disturbed. Then he brought his writing back to Louie at the ranch for her suggestions on how it could be improved.

One day, Muir had an appointment with an editor of *Century* magazine in the Palace Hotel in San Francisco. The editor, Robert Underwood Johnson, used to work at *Scribner's* and had enjoyed Muir's articles. Now he hoped Muir would write for the *Century*.

The meeting got off to a bad start because Muir, who could find his way through mazelike mountain trails, couldn't find his way through the hotel's "artificial canyons." Muir suggested that they camp out in Yosemite and continue the discussion there.

At that time, only Yosemite Valley and the Mariposa Big Tree Grove were protected in any way. The federal government had granted these areas to California in 1864 for "public use, resort, and recreation." Although Muir's friend Galen Clark, the Yosemite Guardian, worked hard to protect the valley, the state government permitted land to be leased in these areas, and the California State Commission was in charge. One trouble with this arrangement was that people disagreed about what should and shouldn't be permitted in the area. A much larger area around the Yosemite Valley had been given no protection.

When Muir and Johnson reached the valley, they saw that the California State Commission had allowed ranchers to cut down trees to make grazing areas for animals. This was true both in the Yosemite Valley and in the area around it. When Muir saw that the beautiful Tuolumne Meadows were practically bare, he was appalled. Most of the grass and beautiful flowers had been destroyed by the "hoofed locusts."

As the two men talked about the destruction of the natural beauty around them, Muir became tearful. To his great surprise, Johnson found that he was deeply moved by Muir's feeling for the land. Johnson told Muir that he thought the great stretch of land around the valley should become a national park. Both Muir and Johnson knew that Yellowstone had been established in 1872 as the first national park, but Wyoming was then a territory not a state. Could a national park be established in a state? Muir explained that in 1881 he had worked on bills that would have created such a park, but his efforts had failed.

Johnson suggested that the two of them could accomplish a great deal together. He asked Muir to write two articles for the *Century*. One would describe all the wonders of the beautiful Yosemite area. The other would suggest that a national park could be established around Yosemite Valley. In these articles, Muir would make a direct appeal to the American people to protect these areas from destruction. He could even draw a map to suggest its boundaries. Johnson, who knew many important people in Washington, D.C., would go to the nation's capital and enlist their support for this idea of a national park. He promised that if Muir wrote the articles, he would see to it that a bill was introduced before Congress. Neither Muir nor Johnson knew it yet, but together they were planting a seed that would soon flower in the minds of many Americans—a love of the nation's wild natural places and a need to protect them.

When Muir went home, the first piece he wrote was an article for the *San Francisco Bulletin* telling how the California State Commission had permitted the rapid destruction of the valley. "Not one garden accessible [easy to reach] has been spared," he wrote. He suggested that the U.S. government should take charge of all watershed areas. (A watershed area is the whole of a region from which water drains into a particular river or lake.) Then he wrote the two articles for *Century*.

Now Muir was ready to take off for Alaska again. But he had a lingering cough. When he told his doctor that he planned to go to Alaska, the doctor said, "If you go on this journey in your condition, you'll pay for it with your life."

"If I don't go, I'll pay for it with my life," Muir responded.

Muir understood his own health better than the doctor did. He headed north in the middle of July, and his cough gradually disappeared. He reached Muir Glacier, the glacier that is now named for him, and made a camp on it. Then he went out exploring with a sled and a bearskin-lined sleeping bag. One day as he sat enjoying the sights and sounds of the glacier, he wrote in his journal, "To dine with a glacier on a sunny day is a glorious thing."

Alaska's glaciers are always changing. Huge chunks fall off them into the sea, making loud crashes as they break away and fall. These glaciers also move much faster than those in the Sierra Nevada. Huge crevasses develop in different parts of the glacier. In fact, there was always a possibility that a crevasse would form between the time Muir went out exploring and the time he returned to his camp.

Traveling alone, Muir had many near brushes with death. In one place, which he named Howling Valley, he heard wolves and had to hold them off with an ice ax. In another, he slipped and tumbled down a snow hill. Ravens circled above hoping he would become their meal, but he said to them, "Not yet." Several days later, he crashed through thin ice and found himself floundering in a crevasse filled with ice-cold water. He managed to crawl out using his ax and rope. Then he removed his clothes and climbed into his bearskin sleeping bag. Fortunately, the boat that had left Muir on the glacier returned a day early—just after his chilly bath—and took him back on board.

When Muir returned to California in September, he learned that many people were talking about his idea for a national park. Many newspaper editorials supported his articles. When a bill was introduced in Congress, Americans sent in letters, telegrams, and petitions demanding that the bill be made a law.

Some people, however, were against making the area around Yosemite Valley a national park. These were the opponents of the bill. A few of these people spread lies about John Muir, saying that he himself had chopped down trees for logs when he worked for Hutchings. Muir sat down and calmly wrote a letter explaining that he had used wood only from trees that had already fallen.

Muir's opponents lost their smear campaign against him. Congress passed the bill. Then President Benjamin Harrison, who was in favor of the national park, signed the bill creating Yosemite National Park on October 1, 1890. A few days before that, land just south of Yosemite was made into Sequoia National Park. (Actually both Yosemite and Sequoia were called forest reserves in the laws that established them. They were not officially parks until 1905). The 1890 laws, however, didn't say who would protect the parks.

Shortly after Yosemite became a national park, Muir again had to face serious family problems. At the end of October, Dr. Strentzel died. John, Louie, Wanda, and Helen moved out of the ranch house and into the Big House so that Louie could help care for her mother. They now needed someone to manage Dr. Strentzel's part of the ranch. About six months later, John Reid, Muir's brother-in-law, came to California with Margaret to take charge of the ranch.

A year later, David Muir found himself in trouble. He and a partner had successfully operated a store in Portage, Wisconsin. But the partner had made some poor decisions and the store was now bankrupt. David and his partner owed money to the neighboring farmers and suppliers whose products had stocked the store. These people were furious.

Muir went to Portage and calmed everybody down. He promised that if David could leave for California, he would see to it that all were paid the money David owed them.

Muir offered his brother part of the ranch to farm. They would share the profits. This would help both of them. John wouldn't have to worry about the ranch, and David could earn the money he needed to pay off his debts. (In time, David paid back all the money he owed to the people in Portage.)

Muir could once again turn his attention to saving the Sierra Nevada. Robert Underwood Johnson had been urging him to form a group of Californians who would be willing to work to save the mountain range from destruction. In 1892, Muir and his friends started the Sierra Club. It was devoted to protecting the land, forests, and watersheds of the Sierra Nevada.

The Sierra Club was established just in time. Some people were trying to get Congress to take away half of the land that had been set aside for Yosemite National Park. A bill reducing the size of the park had already been passed in the House of Representatives. The Sierra Club now had to fight to keep the Senate from passing it.

Muir proved to be the club's best weapon. He spoke to many people and gave interviews in newspapers and magazines. He made the American people care about protecting their wilderness areas. In the end, the Senate didn't pass the bill, and Yosemite National Park was saved.

With all the traveling and writing Muir did, it's amazing that he still had time for his family. Yet he did. His wife encouraged his efforts and understood that he had important work to do, and his children adored him. One of their favorite evening pastimes was listening to their father tell Paddy Grogan stories. These were stories Muir had invented about the adventures of an Irish lad named Paddy Grogan and the kangaroo he rode around Australia. Adults were also fascinated by these tales, and they urged John to write a

*John Muir with some members of the Sierra Club. He helped found
the organization in 1892 and became its first president.*

book of them. He never found the time. Many people who had heard the stories felt that a wonderful part of children's literature had been lost forever.

Muir often visited his friend William Keith in San Francisco. The two friends had been planning a trip to Europe for many years. Finally, Keith announced that he and his wife were going. Muir said he would join them. Keith left first, and Muir followed. Although both of them finally reached Europe, they ended up traveling separately.

When John Muir arrived in New York to depart for Europe, he tried to hide out in a quiet hotel. But Robert Underwood Johnson wouldn't allow that. Many people in the East had heard of Muir and hoped to meet him. Johnson wanted to introduce Muir to many famous people. He hoped these new friends would encourage Muir and support his efforts to save the wilderness.

Together, they went to many lunches and dinners. John Muir met many famous people, including the writers Mark Twain and Rudyard Kipling, and the electrical engineer, inventor, and scientist Nikola Tesla.

The people Muir met took an immediate liking to him. He was a wonderful storyteller, and he had a good sense of humor. He also had a knack for describing the wilderness in such a way that others could imagine its attraction. Often he told the story of his adventures with the dog Stickeen on the glacier. It was a favorite. Whenever he talked about Stickeen, people were fascinated. Servants would linger behind doors to hear about the brave little dog.

At this time, Muir also met James Pinchot. Pinchot said that his son Gifford was studying forestry in Europe. (Several years later, John Muir and Gifford Pinchot would meet and find themselves on opposite sides of major conservation battles.)

Muir left for Europe at the end of July 1893. One of the first places he stopped was Scotland. He visited his hometown of Dunbar and looked up a cousin who still lived there. He also saw Agnes Purns, the girl who so many years ago had beaten him in the race up Davel Brae.

The poverty Muir saw in Dunbar disturbed him. After he returned to the United States, he sent a yearly Christmas gift of money. Part of it was for his cousin. The rest was given to the poor. He continued to do this until his death.

Muir also spent time studying the glaciers of Norway and its fjords—narrow inlets of the sea between cliffs or steep slopes. In Switzerland, he visited his old friend Sir Joseph Hooker, who had visited him during the early days when he was guiding important visitors around Yosemite.

Muir was surprised to learn that he was famous even in Europe. He came home with a new understanding. The only way the wilderness could be saved, he decided, was by making people love it. He would use his writing to accomplish this.

9

The Fight for Recession

O n his way home from Europe, Muir had a new reason for wanting to get back to his writing. The articles and books he wrote would bring the wilderness to life for people who had never seen it. Once they learned to love it as he did, they too would want to save it. He was eager to get back to California.

When Muir reached New York, he found a telegram from Louie waiting for him. It said that before returning home he should go to Washington, D.C., to meet the new secretary of the interior. If Muir could speak to him, it might help conservation efforts. Muir spoke to the new secretary and to everyone else he thought might help him with Yosemite and other forest areas. Then he returned to Martinez.

For his first book, *The Mountains of California*, Muir rewrote many of his magazine articles. These articles had to be brought up to date, and his religiously enthusiastic language had to be toned down. Robert Underwood Johnson gave Muir a lot of help with the articles, but the greatest help came from Louie. Each morning Muir would write for several hours. Then he read what he wrote to Louie, and she offered suggestions before he went back to work.

The Mountains of California was published in 1894, and within a few weeks its first printing was sold out. This book did a great deal to help people who cared about conservation focus on the work that had to be done. In it Muir wrote about *ecology*—the relationship between living things and their surroundings—long before the word came into popular use. His works explained how events at the mountaintops affected what happened in the valleys. He described the changes that had taken place over the past centuries and the very rapid changes that were taking place as a result of human activity. He pictured nature as a dynamic system—always changing. As a result of Muir's book, many people became interested in saving the forests of the United States.

A group made up of leading scientists who wanted to save the forests and watersheds was formed. It was called the National Forestry Commission. John Muir was invited to be a member, but he said he would rather be an adviser.

In June 1896, Muir had another one of his premonitions. Something made him feel that he should visit his mother if he wanted to see her again. He took the next train to Portage. Before going, he sent telegrams to his sister Mary and his brother Danny. Danny was a doctor and didn't believe in his brother's premonitions, so he didn't go.

When Muir arrived, his sister Sarah cried, "Oh, John, surely God has sent you. Mother is terribly ill!"

Anne Muir had fallen sick just a few hours before her son arrived. He sent another telegram, along with travel money, to Danny urging him to come. Soon Anne Muir's health seemed to be improving. Many years later, Muir described his premonitions, "what the Scotch called second sight." He said that there is "a basis of truth, founded on natural laws, which perhaps some day we may discover."

Muir remembered that Harvard University wanted to give him an honorary degree on June 24. He had turned it down because he hadn't planned to travel to Massachusetts. Now he realized it wouldn't be difficult to get to Harvard from Wisconsin.

Muir left for Cambridge, Massachusetts. On June 23, 1896, he received a telegram saying that his mother had died. He wired back that he would be back in Wisconsin in time for the funeral. He received his degree and returned to Portage by the next train.

Since he was already in the Midwest, Muir joined the National Forestry Commission in Chicago and traveled west with them. Charles Sprague Sargent was the chairman. Gifford Pinchot, the son of the man Muir had met in New York several years earlier, was another member of the commission. The commission found that huge areas of forest had been spoiled. The "hoofed locusts" had destroyed most of the plants around Oregon's beautiful Crater Lake.

Many big companies didn't want the government to put aside any more land for national forests or parks. To get around the law, they sent all their workers out to file claims for land that was about to be declared national parks. Then the companies took over the land from their workers.

What was especially upsetting was the discovery that even the national forest reserves were being damaged. The commission knew that it would have to find a better way to protect the land the government meant to save. John Muir and Charles Sprague Sargent thought the army should guard the forests. Gifford Pinchot thought there should be a civilian group of forest guards, similar to those he had seen in Europe.

The members of the commission didn't agree on everything, but they did come up with four important recommendations:

1. Thirteen new reservations should be created in eight western states.
2. All the timber and mining laws that led to fraud and robbery should be changed or eliminated.
3. Forests should be scientifically managed to ensure a permanent supply of timber.
4. The government should create two new national parks—the Grand Canyon and Mount Rainier, including the area around each of them.

President Grover Cleveland thought the commission's ideas were excellent. On George Washington's birthday, he signed an executive order declaring that the thirteen reservations would be set aside.

The companies that opposed this program got people to send letters and telegrams to Congress protesting. Even though President Cleveland was nearing the end of his term of office, some people tried to impeach him, that is, remove him from office. When they didn't succeed, the Senate added a rider—an extra amendment—to a bill in Congress. The purpose of this rider was to undo the executive order that had put aside the thirteen new reservations. President Cleveland threatened to veto the entire bill.

Once again, Muir's pen would be needed to assist the conservation cause. Sargent recommended Muir's writing to the *Atlantic Monthly*, one of the country's leading magazines. Muir's first article for the magazine was "The American Forests." In this article he gave the magazine's readers information from the Forestry Report that the government hadn't made public. He told the public that "Timber thieves...are seldom convicted, for the good reason that most of the jurors who try such cases are themselves as guilty as those on trial." He explained that more than $36 million worth of timber was stolen from the government, and only $478,000 had been recovered. He wrote that any citizen could get 160 acres of timber land by paying $2.50 an acre. Just one tree on that acre was often worth more than $100. He ended the article by saying:

> Any fool can destroy trees. They cannot run away; and if they could, they would still be destroyed—chased and hunted down....Few that fell [cut down] trees plant them....It took more than three thousand years to make some of the trees in these Western woods,—trees that are still standing in perfect strength and beauty, waving and singing in the mighty forests of the Sierra. Through all the wonderful, eventful centuries since Christ's time—and long before that—God has cared for these trees, saved them from drought, disease, avalanches,...but he cannot save them from fools,—only Uncle Sam can do that.

In 1897, Alaska and its glaciers were again calling to John Muir. On this trip he found that the northern country was filled with people bound for the Klondike Gold Rush in nearby Canada. He thought the prospectors' desire for gold made them behave in a beastly fashion.

On his way to Alaska, Muir happened to stop over in

Seattle, Washington. While there he learned that a newspaper had quoted Gifford Pinchot as saying that sheep did little harm to the reserves. Muir couldn't believe this. He knew that Pinchot had seen the same things he had seen at Crater Lake and other areas. Pinchot himself had even admitted that the sheep did a lot of harm.

Muir later confronted Pinchot in a hotel lobby with the newspaper in his hand. Muir did not know that there were reporters watching them, and their conversation would become public.

"Are you correctly quoted here?" he asked.

Pinchot said that he was. Muir told Pinchot that he didn't want to have anything more to do with him. This was the beginning of a long series of public disagreements between the two men.

When Muir returned from Alaska, Louie's mother was close to death. Her death two weeks later was a severe blow to both Muir and his wife. He had come to look upon Mrs. Strentzel as a second mother.

In his second article for the *Atlantic Monthly*, Muir attacked Gifford Pinchot's ideas. "Wild Parks and Forest Reservations of the West" told people that the parks were there for them to enjoy. Between August 1897 and September 1901, the *Atlantic Monthly* published ten articles by John Muir about the forests, animals, trees, and water. Later Muir made them into a book called *Our National Parks*. It was published in 1901 and dedicated to Charles Sprague Sargent, "steadfast [firm and loyal] lover and defender of our country's forests," who had been the chairman of the National Forestry Commission.

John Muir was now traveling a great deal. He returned to some of the areas he had explored during his thousand-mile walk in 1867 from Indiana to the Gulf of Mexico and was sad to see that they had not recovered from the blight of the Civil War. After stopping in Washington, D.C., Muir went on to Florida, and he visited Mr. and Mrs. Hodgson. (They were the kind couple who had nursed him back to health at the end of his walk to the Gulf.) When Mrs. Hodgson realized who Muir was, she exclaimed, "My John Muir!"

One of the most interesting trips Muir took at this time was as a member of the 1899 Harriman Expedition. Edward Henry Harriman was a wealthy owner of railroads and shipping lines. Harriman arranged a voyage to Alaska and Siberia and invited leading scientists, artists, and photographers to join his family. John Muir, the expert on glaciers, was asked to be one of the members of this party.

The Muir family on the front porch of their house near Martinez, where they ran a large fruit farm. From left to right: Daughters Wanda and Helen; their mother, Louie; and their father, John.

Muir made many new friends on this trip. One of them was Harriman himself. Harriman's help would later prove to be very important in the battle for conservation. John Burroughs, one of the nation's leading naturalists, was another. Their joking friendship led people to call the two men the "Two Johnnies."

When the expedition reached Alaska, Muir saw many sights he had seen before. But he noticed that great changes had taken place in Glacier Bay since his first voyage in 1879. A photographer and a mapmaker recorded what they saw at Glacier Bay. Shortly after the Harriman Expedition left Alaska, an earthquake struck Glacier Bay. The maps and photographs helped scientists compare the area before and after the earthquake.

When the ship reached Taylor Bay, Muir stood at the rail and thought of the brave dog Stickeen. Then the expedition discovered a new fjord and five new glaciers. John Muir named the fjord and one glacier—Harriman Fjord and Harriman Glacier—in honor of the expedition's host.

When the twelve-volume book *The Harriman Alaska Expedition* was published, it included an article entitled "Pacific Coast Glaciers" by John Muir.

In 1901, President McKinley had been assassinated, and the vice-president, Theodore Roosevelt, became the new president of the United States. Roosevelt told a member of the Harriman Expedition that he would be interested in learning about abuses in government programs. When Muir learned of this, he wrote to the president. Muir suggested that the country needed a Bureau of Forestry. He was glad to learn that President Roosevelt had included the preservation of forests and water areas in his first message to Congress.

Then a letter arrived from Robert Underwood Johnson.

Johnson wrote that President Roosevelt wanted Muir to guide him through Yosemite. Muir almost turned the invitation down because he was planning a world tour with Charles Sprague Sargent. Without mentioning the president, Muir got Sargent to agree to postpone their trip. Plans went forward for the president's visit in 1903.

On their first night in Yosemite, President Theodore Roosevelt and John Muir camped out in the Mariposa Grove, while the president's assistants remained in the background. The next day, the two men took their horses to Glacier Point and camped there. Afterward President Roosevelt said, "This has been the grandest day of my life! One I shall long remember."

On their third night, the two men camped out under El Capitan without a tent. Theodore Roosevelt was delighted to wake up and find his blanket covered with snow.

Muir's camping out with the president advanced the cause of conservation. Muir had a chance to tell Roosevelt about timber thieves and people who spoiled the forests. He also discussed the idea of *recession*—having California give the Yosemite Valley back to the federal government so that it could be included in the Yosemite National Park.

Roosevelt, who had encouraged conservation when he was the governor of New York State, agreed with many of Muir's ideas. The president understood that California depended on a reliable water supply and on preserving its forests. Roosevelt said, "We are not building this country of ours for a day. It is to last through the ages."

Roosevelt also made things easier for Muir and Sargent when they finally left on their world tour. He told American embassies around the world to offer any assistance the men needed. They began in Europe and stopped to see some of the great museums. But for Muir, the greatest attraction

President Theodore Roosevelt and John Muir at Glacier Point overlooking Yosemite Valley. Roosevelt's famous visit to Yosemite took place in 1903.

everywhere was the forests. They saw the great forests of Russia as well as those of Finland.

Muir became sick, but he was also worried because there had been no letters from home. In Moscow, he sent a cable to Louie. She sent one back saying, "All's well. Loving greetings!"

After visiting Siberia and Manchuria, Sargent had to return home, but Muir wanted to continue his world tour. Edward Henry Harriman instructed his shipping offices to smooth the way for Muir, who went on to China and India. At this point in his travels, he began to have an uncomfortable feeling about his daughter Helen and cabled home again. The answer was again "All's well." His family didn't tell him that Helen had several severe bouts of pneumonia. Muir continued on to Egypt and then to Australia and New Zealand.

He had been traveling for a little more than a year when he decided to return home. His two daughters greeted him at the dock and took him back to their mother at the ranch.

John Muir had new work ahead of him. In the autumn of 1904, the movement for recession of Yosemite Valley grew more serious. Recession meant that the state of California would give Yosemite Valley and Mariposa Grove back to the national government. The Sierra Club began to work hard for this objective. The nearby areas outside the valley and the giant sequoia grove had already become a national park in 1890.

Some Californians who were against recession thought the recessionists were traitors. They felt giving the valley back to the federal government would damage California's public image. Other opponents of recession had been abusing the forests or waterways. They knew that the federal government would crack down on their activities.

The bill that the Sierra Club backed passed in the California Assembly, but the California Senate faced a big battle. Most people expected the railroad interests to oppose recession. But John Muir turned to Edward Henry Harriman for help and received it. With Harriman's assistance, enough members of the railroad group backed recession, and the bill was passed in the California Senate.

Only half the battle had been won, though. Now the United States Congress had to accept the grant back. This fight promised to be more difficult. Once again, Muir turned to Harriman for help, and once more Harriman's influence made the difference. Congress passed the bill. The president then signed the recession bill into law on June 6, 1906. Now the entire Yosemite area would be managed by the federal government.

During the previous year, Muir's daughter Helen had been sick again. The doctor advised the Muirs to take her to the desert. In May, John and Wanda took Helen to Arizona, where they hoped she would recover.

While they were there, a letter arrived from his wife Louie near the end of June. She wrote that she had been sick but was now fine. Three days later, Muir received a telegram asking them to come home.

When Muir and Wanda returned to the ranch, they learned that Louie had a tumor on her lung. She died on August 6, 1905, and was buried on the ranch.

Muir was devastated by his wife's death. They had been married for twenty-five years, and he loved and depended on her.

Wanda returned to Arizona with her father. There she nursed him and her sister back to health. Muir continued to feel lost. He couldn't write. He needed his wife's help and encouragement. What would he do without her?

10

The Last Battle

John Muir was sixty-eight years old when his wife, Louie, died. They had been married for twenty-five years, and he missed her grievously. For more than a year after her death, he was unable to write.

His daughters helped him get through this depressing time. Wanda nursed Helen back to health. Then both young women often went out into the Arizona desert on horseback. Sometimes their father rode with them.

As John was riding with Helen one day, he noticed what seemed to be logs of trees lying about the desert. But there were no trees growing in the area. He got off his horse to inspect the logs.

What Muir discovered was petrified wood, a kind of fossil in which minerals slowly over millions of years replace the original wood. What was left were stones with the shapes and grains of wood. These fossils were blue, so the area Muir found became known as the Blue Forest. Later he came across areas that contained petrified wood of different colors.

Nature was presenting Muir with another mystery that he wanted to understand. He set about learning everything he could about petrified wood. He bought books and went to the university library. He also wrote to other scientists. Then he began to worry about the future of his discovery. People passing through the area had already begun to cut up logs of petrified wood to sell as souvenirs. Muir wanted to preserve the area.

Fortunately, Congress had just passed a new law making places that had scientific or historic importance into national monuments. At Muir's urging, President Theodore Roosevelt declared the Petrified Forest a national monument. Later the protected area was enlarged.

John Muir writes in his journal during his visit to Arizona's petrified "forest." The area became a national monument in 1906. It was made a national park in 1962.

Muir also advised Roosevelt to set aside part of the Grand Canyon as a national monument. Monuments are land areas that can be established by presidential order. National parks, however, require laws passed by Congress. People who wanted to use the Grand Canyon for commercial purposes challenged this order in the United States Supreme Court. The Court ruled that making the area a national monument was legal. (Later, under President Woodrow Wilson in 1919, the Grand Canyon National Park was established. This covered a much greater area.)

The Muir girls had become adults. Wanda, in her mid-twenties, was a student at the University of California. There she met Thomas Rae Hanna, a civil engineer. They were married in June 1906. The newlyweds moved into an adobe house near the entrance to the ranch.

Muir and Helen settled into the Big House and he began to write again. Helen learned to type so she could help her father with his writing. Each afternoon after the work was done, the two of them went out to look at flowers and birds. Their dog (named Stickeen, after the dog Muir had met in Alaska) usually went with them.

Helen shared her father's interest in mechanical things. Because she especially loved railroad cars and engines, her father arranged for her to ride in the cab of trains whenever they traveled. She even learned to drive a train.

Helen was a great favorite among the railroad men. They had a special "rooster whistle" sound they made whenever a train went past the Big House. Then Helen would come out and wave to them. Once she shocked her aunt Margaret Reid by leaving a dinner party to go out and wave to the train men. When the fruits on the ranch were ripe, Muir and Helen often gave baskets of them to the railroad men.

The Hetch Hetchy Valley. The dispute over whether or not to flood this valley to provide water and electricity was Muir's last great preservation battle.

During the early part of the twentieth century, many people were beginning to install electricity and telephones in their homes. John Muir did not. In the evenings, the Muir family continued to enjoy sitting in the warm glow of candlelight and firelight. When friends came over, the house echoed with the sounds of good-natured joking, singing and storytelling. Muir always told good stories and so did many of his friends.

Despite the contentment at home, trouble was developing in the Sierra Nevada, and Muir would soon find himself in the middle of a serious fight for the wilderness.

The fight would be about the Hetch Hetchy Valley of the Tuolumne River. This beautiful valley was considered to be a "twin" to Yosemite Valley. Hetch Hetchy was now part of the Yosemite National Park. On one camping trip, the artist William Keith told Muir that "in picturesque beauty and charm Hetch Hetchy surpassed even Yosemite."

For many years, San Francisco had worried about its water supply. A private company was the only supplier of the city's water. The city's leaders believed it was dangerous to rely on a single source for something that was so essential. San Franciscans also worried that they wouldn't get enough water for their growing city. The mayor wanted to use the water from the Hetch Hetchy Valley. A dam could be built to create a reservoir—a lake to store water—where the beautiful valley was. He also wanted the city to acquire inexpensive hydroelectric power—power generated from the energy of falling water.

James D. Phelan, who was then mayor of San Francisco, secretly had a survey done of the Hetch Hetchy Valley and nearby Lake Eleanor. In 1901, Mayor Phelan even had bills passed quietly in the United States Congress to allow San Francisco to use Hetch Hetchy water.

Each request was turned down by the secretary of the interior. The secretary said that the development of the reservoirs San Francisco wanted would destroy the scenic areas of the park. The city of San Francisco then appealed to President Roosevelt, who turned the matter over to Gifford Pinchot. Pinchot was then chief forester in the newly established Forest Service.

Pinchot and Muir had very different ideas about natural resources. Pinchot wanted to *conserve* them, or save them for continual use. Muir wanted to *preserve* them—that is, to keep them as close as possible to the way nature made them. Miners, lumber-mill owners, and cattle owners sided with Pinchot. They wanted to be able to use the national forests and parks for commercial purposes. Many scientists and nature lovers sided with John Muir. They wanted to preserve the wild areas for scenery and recreation.

The two groups had argued for years without feeling any sense of urgency. Then the San Francisco earthquake changed the nature of the argument. Early in the morning of April 18, 1906, San Francisco endured the worst earthquake recorded up to that time in the United States. Stoves were knocked over and fires raced through the city's streets. Water was hard to get, and the citizens felt they had more reason than ever to demand Hetch Hetchy water.

Some observers pointed out that the problem was not that San Francisco had too little water after the earthquake but that the water wasn't being directed where it was needed. Instead, it was leaking into the streets and turning the soil into mud.

Gifford Pinchot wrote a letter to San Francisco officials sympathizing with their plight after the earthquake. In his letter he also said that he hoped San Francisco's people would get "a water supply from the Yosemite National Park."

The Sierra Club members themselves couldn't come to an agreement on the Hetch Hetchy water issue. Some thought that the needs of San Francisco came first. Others believed Muir was right when he said the city could get enough water from other sources. After those who wanted to save Hetch Hetchy won a vote that was taken, about fifty members left the club.

Muir had been working with conservationists throughout the country to save Hetch Hetchy. To gain support for the cause, he gave speeches and wrote many letters, telegrams, and pamphlets asking the nation to save the valley.

During this time, Muir worried about saving his daughter as well as the Hetch Hetchy Valley. Helen was sick again. A doctor told her that she would need two years in the desert in order to get well. Sadly, Muir helped her move to Daggett, California, near the Mohave Desert. There he built a cabin for her and arranged for her to have a nurse. Then he sent her the dog Stickeen and her horse, Sniffpony.

Some victories and surprises lay in store for conservationists. In 1907, to the delight of many, President Roosevelt set aside vast areas of land to be used as national parks. He also made some of the existing national parks larger.

John Muir wrote a personal letter to Roosevelt about Hetch Hetchy, but the president continued to leave decisions about the valley to Gifford Pinchot, the man who said that a reservoir and dam would have no effect on the scenic value of the Sierra Nevada.

After a while, it became clear that saving Hetch Hetchy would depend in part on who was president and who was secretary of the interior. Each time there was a change in either or both offices, the two sides had to present their arguments all over again.

In May a "Conservation Conference" was arranged at the White House. Pinchot helped to arrange it, and to the surprise of many, John Muir, Charles Sprague Sargent, and other leaders in conservation weren't invited. Robert Underwood Johnson attended as a member of the press and protested the absence of John Muir and others. The reply was that there was "no room" for them.

In 1909, William Howard Taft succeeded Theodore Roosevelt as president. To many people's surprise, he appointed a new secretary of the interior, Richard Ballinger. Gifford Pinchot was furious. Ballinger showed signs of opposing the damming of the Hetch Hetchy Valley, and Pinchot wanted both the dam and the reservoir.

Hearings were held in Washington, D.C. James Phelan,

the former mayor of San Francisco, was in favor of the dam. He also brought up all the old lies accusing Muir of cutting down Yosemite trees during the 1870s. But when he was questioned, Phelan admitted that there were "more than a dozen" other water sources available. Johnson wrote to Muir and told him that he thought they would win.

Later, in September, President Taft asked Muir to be his guide during a visit to Yosemite. Hoping that it would help Hetch Hetchy, Muir accepted.

President Taft enjoyed teasing Muir, and Muir responded in the same spirit. Taft looked around and said, "Now that would be a fine place for a dam!"

"A dam!" Muir exclaimed. "But the man who would dam that would be damning himself!"

At first the two men were surrounded by reporters. When Muir had a chance to talk to the president privately, he brought out his collection of maps and charts. On them he had drawn plans for roads and trails that could connect the different scenic areas of the park, including the Hetch Hetchy Valley. The president then asked Muir if he would guide Richard Ballinger, secretary of the interior, through Yosemite. Muir did so and spoke out against damming the Hetch Hetchy Valley. He explained that he thought the water from Lake Eleanor would be enough. He also pointed out that Lake Eleanor was far less scenic than Hetch Hetchy. A board set up to study Lake Eleanor and the Hetch Hetchy Valley agreed with Muir. Its members decided that Lake Eleanor's water would be enough.

Gifford Pinchot was furious. He encouraged several magazines to write articles attacking Ballinger. Pressure was put on President Taft to dismiss Ballinger, but Taft stood by him. In the end it was Pinchot who was dismissed.

Meanwhile, there was exciting news in the Muir family.

Helen was marrying Buel A. Funk, a man who lived near Daggett, and they would make their home in that area.

Several years earlier, in 1905, near the California coast, a man named William Kent bought a piece of land called Redwood Canyon to the south of Mount Tamalpais. He bought the land because he loved the great coast redwood trees that grew there. He wanted to save them from being cut down. He told his wife that the purchase would be worthwhile even if they lost the money and saved the trees.

Kent tried to give the land and its trees to several organizations as a gift, but nobody would accept it. In 1907, a water company sued to take over the land and use it as a reservoir. Kent was worried. Then he remembered that Congress had passed a law making scientific and historic areas into national monuments. Through the help of politicians, including Gifford Pinchot, Kent had Redwood Canyon declared a national monument in 1908.

President Roosevelt wanted to name the canyon Kent Monument, but Kent refused. He had spent a great deal of time reading and admiring the writings of John Muir, and he insisted the area be called Muir Woods.

John Muir later sent a letter to Kent thanking him for the honor. In it he wrote: "This is the best tree-lovers' monument that could be found. You have done me a great honor and I am proud of it."

In the summer of 1908, the Harriman family invited Muir to their lodge in Oregon. At first he turned down the invitation because he was writing a book, but Edward Henry Harriman insisted.

The group at the lodge enjoyed spending the evenings telling stories to one another. Muir, of course, was one of the best storytellers. One evening Harriman had an idea. His secretary could follow Muir around and take down every-

John Muir and one of California's coast redwoods in Muir Forest just north of San Francisco.

thing he said in shorthand. Then Muir could use the typewritten notes to write his books. Muir thought Thomas Price, Harriman's secretary, was a nuisance because he trailed him all the time. Yet the more than a thousand pages that Price typed became the basis for an important book, Muir's autobiography—*The Story of My Boyhood and Youth*.

Harriman died about a year after this gathering, and Muir truly missed his friend. He had come to realize that wealthy people can use their money and power for good or evil. Harriman, he felt, had used his for good. John Muir wrote a moving tribute to his friend.

Yale University wrote to Muir early in 1910 telling him that the school wanted to give him an honorary degree. He accepted. Then his sister Margaret Reid died, and he had to postpone his acceptance of the degree.

By now, Muir's daughter Wanda had two sons, Strentzel and John. Helen had one, whom she named Muir. Their grandfather spent as much time with them as he could.

Slowly many of John Muir's old friends were dying. William Keith died in April 1911. Muir thought about his own life and remembered that he had always wanted to go to South America. This might be his last chance, he decided. Friends were horrified at the thought of his going into the jungle at his age.

Muir told them, "God will take care of me and bring me home safely."

Before leaving for his trip, Muir stopped in New York and Washington and gave speeches asking people to save Hetch Hetchy. Then he went to Yale to receive his honorary degree. He also finished the work on two of his books, *The Story of My Boyhood and Youth* and *The Yosemite*.

In August 1911, Muir left for South America. First he sailed up the Amazon River. Then he sailed up the Rio

Negro looking for a large white-flowered plant called *Victoria regia*. To everybody's amazement, he crawled around the tangled vines and fallen trees of the jungle in his search. He never found it, but he continued to travel around the continent.

In Buenos Aires, Argentina, many people wanted to meet the famous nature writer. Muir was amazed to discover that he was well known so far from his own country. He spent most of his time out in the country looking for a tree he had read about. It was called the monkey-puzzle tree, and its branches made many loops and tangles. Nobody knew where to find it, but Muir figured out a way to track it down. He thought about the kind of soil, temperature, and water the tree needed. Then he looked for a region that had the right land and climate. He found the tree and insisted on sleeping under it.

President Taft knew that Muir was traveling and made sure that the U.S. State Department looked after his friend. As a result, people everywhere helped Muir along the way.

Muir had told his friends that he was going to South America. But he had not told them that he intended to go to Africa as well. In January 1912, he landed at Cape Town, South Africa. He traveled north, looking for the baobab tree. One hotel owner said nobody had ever asked for baobabs before and he didn't know what they were. Finally, a young African boy took Muir to some of the trees. These huge trees have many trunks. One tree can make a whole forest. Muir also visited the famous Victoria Falls and compared it with the falls at Yosemite Valley.

By March, Muir was back in the United States. Despite his friends' concern for him, he had not been sick for even a day during his trip.

He visited Helen and her son Muir, who were living in

Hollywood. Then he saw Wanda, and her three sons, Strentzel, John, and baby Richard. Helen's second son, Stanley, was born in July.

Muir then returned to the ranch to finish his book *Travels in Alaska*. Often when he was supposed to be working, he walked across the ranch to play with Wanda's boys. He also met his friend John Swett each morning at the place where their two ranches met. The two old friends usually sat on Swett's porch and talked.

For a while, it seemed that the Hetch Hetchy battle had quieted, but matters were about to change. A hearing held in November 1912 ended by denying San Francisco a "power and water reservoir." But changes were about to take place in the White House.

Another presidential election was coming up. Taft was running again as a Republican. Theodore Roosevelt was running as an independent, for a party nicknamed the Bull Moose party. Gifford Pinchot was one of Roosevelt's main supporters. Woodrow Wilson was the Democrat running against Taft and Roosevelt. John Muir thought Taft would be best for the forests.

Wilson won. The person he appointed secretary of the interior turned out to be the man who had served as San Francisco's attorney.

The Hetch Hetchy fight in Congress began with a sneaky move. In August, the members of Congress were told that the Hetch Hetchy bill wouldn't come up until December. When many of the lawmakers left town for vacation, the supporters of the bill rushed it through the House of Representatives on September 3. The remaining fight would take place in the Senate.

The people who wanted to preserve Hetch Hetchy mounted a campaign. But in December the bill passed the

John Muir's efforts led to the saving of millions of acres as forest reserves, national parks, and wilderness areas.

Senate. The only hope now was that President Wilson would veto the bill. He didn't. Eventually, at twice the $50 million cost that was estimated, the beautiful Hetch Hetchy Valley was flooded with 175 feet of water. The mountain water ran through pipes into San Francisco.

John Muir had been exhausted by the fight. He felt great sorrow over the loss. Conservationists throughout the nation were shocked. Many people felt as John Muir did— the national parks were not supposed to be spoiled.

The conservationists now had another goal. They wanted to see a National Park Service created to take care of all the parks. John Muir lent his support to this effort as well, but he didn't live to see it. In 1916, William Kent, the man who donated Muir Woods, became a member of Congress. It was he who introduced the bill for the National Park Service that became law.

John Muir was losing many of his friends. In August 1913, John Swett died. The two old friends had received a great honor just before that. In May of that year, the University of California had given them both honorary degrees.

Muir returned to the ranch to finish *Travels in Alaska*. He spent time playing with Wanda's four sons. (Robert Hanna was born in 1914.) It was some time before he was able to visit Helen and her new baby John.

For reasons nobody understood, Muir decided to re-decorate the Big House and install electricity. Then, in December, he went to visit Helen at Daggett. There was a bitter cold when he arrived. Shortly afterward, he fainted. He had pneumonia. Helen rushed him to a hospital in Los Angeles. For a while he seemed better. But on December 24, 1914, John Muir died with the printer's proofs for *Travels in Alaska* on his bed.

John Muir's name can be found in many places in the United States—Mount Muir, Muir Woods, Muir Glacier. Plants, too, have been named after him. His work lives on in the efforts the Sierra Club makes to protect the wilderness. And his daughter Helen made sure that his name would continue in the family. After her husband died, she changed the family name legally. She became Helen Funk Muir, and her sons carried their grandfather's name.

The best tributes to John Muir are the national parks throughout the United States. He is often called the father of our national parks. His articles and speeches helped to make them a reality. John Muir helped us to understand that people need the wilderness for more than commercial reasons. In *Our National Parks*, he wrote:

Thousands of tired, nerve-shaken over-civilized people are beginning to find out that going to the mountains is going home; that wilderness is a necessity; and that mountain parks and reservations are useful not only as fountains of timber and irrigation rivers, but as fountains of life.

Important Dates

1838 John Muir is born on April 21 in Dunbar, Scotland, the son of Daniel and Anne Muir.

1849 The Muir family emigrates to the United States.

1857 The Muir family moves from Fountain Lake to Hickory Hill, both in Wisconsin.

1860 Muir leaves home; wins prize for inventions at State Agricultural Fair in Madison, Wisconsin; meets Jeanne Carr.

1861 Muir enters university at Madison after short stay at Prairie du Chien.

1862 Muir takes time off from university to teach.

1864 Muir botanizes in Canada.

1866 Muir leaves Canada and settles in Indianapolis, Indiana.

1867 Muir leaves industrial work; takes thousand-mile walk to the Gulf of Mexico.

1868 Muir arrives in California; sees Yosemite for the first time.

1871 Muir discovers living glacier in Yosemite; meets Ralph Waldo Emerson at Yosemite.

1872 Muir publishes articles in *Overland Monthly*; stays briefly in Oakland, California.

1876 Muir lives in San Francisco with Swett family.

1879 Muir becomes engaged to Louisa Wanda ("Louie") Strentzel; leaves for Alaska.

1880 Muir marries Louie on April 14, a week before his forty-second birthday.

1881 Annie Wanda Muir is born; Muir returns to Alaska on *Corwin*.

1882 Muir returns home and spends several years as a fruit rancher.

1885 Daniel Muir dies in Kansas City.

1886 Helen Muir is born.

1888 Muir resumes writing and conservation work at Louie's urging; climbs Mount Rainier.

1890 Muir writes articles for *Century*; Dr. Strentzel dies; Yosemite National Park established.

1892 Muir helps establish Sierra Club; elected its first president.

1894 Muir publishes his first book, *The Mountains of California*.

1896 Anne Gilrye Muir dies in Portage; Muir works with Forestry Commission; receives honorary degree from Harvard.

1897 Mrs. Strentzel dies.

1898 Muir receives honorary degree from University of Wisconsin.

1899 Muir joins the Harriman Expedition to Alaska.

1901 Muir writes to President Theodore Roosevelt about conservation; publishes *Our National Parks*.

1903 President Roosevelt camps in Yosemite with Muir.

1905 Louisa Strentzel Muir dies on August 6; Yosemite Valley receded to the United States.

1908 Muir Woods National Monument established; Muir begins fight to save Hetch Hetchy Valley.

1909 Muir publishes *Stickeen*.

1911 Muir publishes *My First Summer in the Sierra*; leaves for South America and Africa; receives honorary degree from Yale.

1913 Muir publishes *Story of My Boyhood and Youth*; loses fight to save Hetch Hetchy; receives honorary degree from University of California.

1914 Muir dies on December 24 in Los Angeles, California, at age 76.

Bibliography

Books About John Muir

Clarke, James M. *The Life and Adventures of John Muir*. San Francisco: Sierra Club Books Edition, 1980.

Cohen, Michael P. *The Pathless Way: John Muir and American Wilderness*. Madison, Wisconsin: University of Wisconsin Press, 1984.

Fox, Stephen. *The American Conservation Movement: John Muir and His Legacy*. Madison, Wisconsin: University of Wisconsin Press, 1985.

* Graves, Charles P. *John Muir*. New York: Thomas Y. Crowell Company, 1973.

Johnson, Robert Underwood. *Remembered Yesterdays*. Boston: Little Brown, 1923.

Jones, Holway. *John Muir and the Sierra Club*. San Francisco: Sierra Club Books Edition, 1965.

* Swift, Hildegarde Hoyt. *From the Eagle's Wings; A Biography of John Muir.* New York: William Morrow and Company, 1962.

Turner, Frederick. *Rediscovering America: John Muir in His Time and Ours.* New York: Viking Penguin, 1985.

Wolfe, Linnie Marsh. *Son of the Wilderness.* Madison, Wisconsin: University of Wisconsin Press, 1980.

Young, Samuel Hall. *Alaska Days with John Muir.* Salem, New Hampshire: Ayer Company Publishers, Reproduction of 1915 ed.

Articles About John Muir

Anderson, Melville: "The Conversation of John Muir." *American Museum Journal*, March 1915.

Johnson, Robert Underwood. "John Muir As I Knew Him" Sierra Club *Bulletin*, January 1916.

———— "Personal Reminiscences of John Muir." *Outlook*, June 3, 1905.

Merriam, C. Hart. "To the Memory of John Muir." Sierra Club *Bulletin*, January 1917.

Patrick, Maribeth. "A Visit With John Muir." Sierra Club *Bulletin*, September/October 1982.

Polos, Nicholas. "The Educational Philosophy of John Swett and John Muir." *Pacific Historian*, Spring 1982.

Stanley, Millie. "John Muir as Remembered by One Who Knew Him." Portage *Daily Reporter*, July 15, 1972.

Books of John Muir's Writings

The Cruise of the Corwin. Scholars Reference Library, no date.

John o' the Mountains. Unpubublished journals, ed. Linnie Marsh Wolfe. Madison, Wisconsin: University of Wisconsin Press, 1979.

My First Summer in the Sierra. New York: Penguin Books, 1987.

The Mountains of California. New York: Penguin Books, 1985.

Our National Parks. Madison, Wisconsin: University of Wisconsin Press, 1981.

* *Stickeen.* Berkeley, California: Heyday Books, 1974.

The Story of My Boyhood and Youth. Boston and New York: The Houghton Mifflin Company, 1912.

Studies in the Sierra. San Francisco: Sierra Club Books, 1950.

A Thousand Mile Walk to the Gulf. Boston: Houghton Mifflin, 1981.

To the Yosemite and Beyond. Madison, Wisconsin: University of Wisconsin Press, 1980.

Travels in Alaska. San Francisco: Sierra Club Books, 1988.

Wilderness Essays. Salt Lake City: Peregrine Smith Books; Gibbs-Smith Publisher, 1980.

The Yosemite. San Francisco: Sierra Club Books, 1988.

* Readers of Pioneers in Change's *John Muir* will find this book particularly readable.

Index

About the Author

Eden Force is a full-time writer and editor of children's books, reference books, and school books. She has written several textbooks, contributed to both children's and adult dictionaries, and written articles for children's encyclopedias. This is her second biography. Eden Force makes her home in New York.

HIRAM HALLE MEM. (POUND RIDGE)

3 1026 10024110 6

B MUIR
Force, Eden
John Muir $13.98